From a very early age, Joanne Hull has had an affinity with animals. During her childhood she discovered that her natural psychic ability gave her a connection with animals that was much more intense than she ever imagined possible. Now a TV favourite after her appearances on *The Wright Stuff* and *The Sharon Osbourne Show*, her gift has helped thousands of people connect with their pets, past and present. Joanne currently lives in Scotland with her fiancé.

By Joanne Hull and available from Headline

The Pet Psychic

Puppy Tales

Heartwarming true stories of man's best friend

Joanne Hull

First published in trade paperback in 2011
by HEADLINE PUBLISHING GROUP

First published in paperback in 2012

1

Cataloguing in Publication Data is available from the British Library

ISBN 978 0 7553 6258 5

Typeset in Dante MT by Palimpsest Book Production Limited,
Falkirk, Stirlingshire

Printed and bound in Great Britain by
Clays Ltd, St Ives plc

Headline's policy is to use papers that are natural, renewable and recyclable
products and made from wood grown in sustainable forests. The logging and
manufacturing processes are expected to conform to the
environmental regulations of the country of origin.

HEADLINE PUBLISHING GROUP
An Hachette UK Company
338 Euston Road
London NW1 3BH

www.headline.co.uk
www.hachette.co.uk

Author's note

Names and personal information have been changed throughout this book to protect the innocent, both the two-legged humans and my furry four-legged friends.

Please be aware that when I use the word 'owner' I do not believe that we own any animals. We only share our lives with them, but the term owner is familiar to all, and therefore will be loosely used throughout this book.

I would like to make it clear that Animal Communication does not replace veterinary treatment in any way. My clients in this book sought advice and treatment for their dogs from a qualified veterinarian before seeking the help of an Animal Communicator such as myself.

Introduction

Puppy Tales was born from the knowledge that many of you adore dogs, just as I do. I truly love puppies. I always have. I love all puppies and dogs, in fact – the good, the bad and the ugly. And I guess you do too. And so I could see nothing better than a book that celebrates the life and times of our furry, wet-nosed, four-legged friends!

My life as the Pet Psychic may seem strange to some folk. Being capable of talking to animals through telepathy and intuition isn't something you hear about every day. But this ability has taken me on the most incredible journey. Yes, this little girl from a small town called Bedworth in Warwickshire has had her dreams come true through the animals around her. How did it happen?

Well, quite simply, I followed my heart. And that heart has been full of these wonderful, comical, wagging-tailed wonders. They have reduced me to tears, made me laugh until my sides hurt and taught me to look at myself in a whole new way. These amazing creatures we know as dogs gave me their 'paw of approval' from day one, with the first wet kiss of the family dog, Blackie, when I was born back in 1971. They have stayed by my side ever since, to help and guide me through times of personal difficulty, stress, excitement and fear.

Today, I am a full-time professional Animal Communicator, working with many different species of animals, from tiny baby mice and long-legged hairy spiders that make me shiver right down my spine in fear to the largest camel and my personal favourites, the horses and donkeys. I have been able to help thousands of people throughout the world communicate with their animals and understand what their pets' needs, wants and likes are, thus creating a perfect partnership with their dogs.

The people who come to me for help with their dogs and puppies are from all walks of life, all professions and beliefs. Each animal I have the honour to read for an owner is different and unique. The owners may be worried about behaviour problems such as chewing, soiling the house or even aggression, or they might be concerned about their pets' anxiety. Whatever the case, I am always able to help in some way. My methods may seem unconventional, perhaps a little odd to some, but one thing's for sure – they work.

It took many years to understand the responsibility I have as a psychic medium, and I still have a lot to learn. Not a day goes past when the dogs and other animals don't teach me something new about their lives. But I know that dogs give their love unconditionally. They serve us and they obey us. Often we rely upon them day to day. And in return, some of us ignore them, abuse them, hurt, torture or sometimes even kill them. If we help just one animal along our journey into Animal Communication, then we will have made a difference. Even if it's as simple as chatting with our own dog and understanding his or her true needs.

Perhaps you too are one of those people who has experienced a unique connection with an animal in your life and now you are eager to learn more about how animals can communicate through telepathic and intuitive means. To many people this is an exciting possibility, like a universal light guiding us into a previously untapped world. Communication with dogs is such a blessing, and I am privileged to be able to share how it is done with my students.

It's simple really. The basis is learning to trust your intuition. Imagine each dog has its own frequency, just like a radio signal. If you can tune your internal antenna to that signal, you can hear the dog, be it in words, emotion or pictures within your mind's eye. It's as easy as that. Anyone can do this. It's an ability we all possess, but it lies dormant in most of us. However, with a little practice it can be brought back to the surface and you can rediscover one of our most amazing abilities – Animal Communication.

So let me take you on a journey into my world and somewhere beyond, where most dog trainers, behaviourists and vets dare not venture, to examine just how incredible dogs are, and tell you some heartwarming true stories – some happy, some sad – from dogs that are living as well as from those that have returned to their owners from beyond the grave to give their humans messages of hope, encouragement and love. I will share with you some of the amazing talks I have been lucky enough to have with dogs over the years, and give you some information that you may not know about our waggy friends.

I truly hope that you enjoy the rest of this book that I have written for you. From me to you, let me introduce *Puppy Tales*!

Chapter One

I have always had an affinity with animals, from as far back as I can remember, and everyone around me noticed it too. People would bring animals to me when they were in need of help and I would know what to do, whether they were injured, rescued or just lost. Whatever the problem was, I seemed to have the answers. In no way was it healing as trained vets do. This was more like emotional healing, giving support, love and energy to those who needed it.

Being around the animals meant everything to me and best of all the animals wanted to be with me too! There was a connection to all, a deep love connection that today I call the 'love link'. It was something I assumed everyone else had – that they understood, respected and loved animals just as much as I did – but over the years growing up I realised that I was slightly different from other children and adults in the way I connected with animals. Not only that, but my ability to help them was unusual too.

Our family's relationship with dogs goes way back through the generations. My mother had dogs before me and my grandparents too, and they were every bit part of the family. Our home was not complete without the good old family dog.

The dog's role in our family varied. Sometimes he was there for us to stroke, pet and confide in. The children played with him and the adults whispered their secrets to him. But he was also meant to protect the family from intruders and deter undesirables from entering the family home. Some of our dogs in earlier years were kept outside in home-made wooden kennels, whilst others slept in the house, be it on the kitchen floor, the sofa or, if they were really lucky, on someone's bed.

I think many cases of dogs sleeping on humans' beds years ago were probably so they could keep their owners warm in winter when there was little heating in most households. I remember sneaking Blackie, our family dog, into my bed like a giant black hot-water bottle. He was so warm and I just loved snuggling up to him. I could see my breath clearly in the air above us, but we encased ourselves completely under the covers, warm and cosy.

Just thinking about those cold nights makes me shiver. As I sit here writing this with the worst winter we have had for years outside my window, I don't think I could manage today with no heating as I did as a child all those years ago.

I remember the time when the heating had broken and all we had was a small brown Calor gas heater in the living room. The bedrooms were utterly freezing! Perhaps that's why today I really don't like a cold house and have to have the heating on constantly.

As I remember it, dogs were mainly cross-breeds when I was a child. Although I do recall my grandparents having pure-bred whippets, most people I knew had the typical Heinz variety dogs, as we called them. This meant that you hadn't actually got a clue what breed the dog was. He might be small with short dumpy legs or tall with a long nose or something in-between.

Our dog Blackie looked more like a cross Labrador and something else, but the Labrador trait came through clearly. He was black, with beautiful dark brown eyes rimmed with black which looked as if someone had lined them with eyeliner. He was slightly grey around the muzzle, which was just a bit longer than the true-bred Labrador. But he was loyal, sweet natured and dependable and I loved him.

Blackie taught me lots of things when I was a young girl, including how to have fun with dogs. I learnt how incredibly patient they can be with children and how they wish to socialise and be part of your games. That was his choice, which always amazes me when I think back to those early years. He would come with me to the park, watching over me and barking in excitement as I swung higher and higher on the park swings. He chased after me as I whizzed down the slide and landed on the grass at the bottom in hysterics, licking my face as if relieved I was still alive. We would do it all over again and again. (My memory of this game is that the grass was always damp and I'd end up not only with a wet bum but also a green one!)

Blackie was the epitome of the family dog. He was trustworthy and fun. When I was at nursery school he would walk me and my mum to the school gates every morning and greet me again at the end of the day. All the children coming out of school used to welcome him, patting his head and saying hello. Some of his favourites even gave him big slobbery hugs and kisses. All the while his tail never stopped wagging in delight and friendliness. He loved it.

I have many fond memories of Blackie. He will be in my heart for ever. His love and companionship whilst I was growing up paved the way for my love of dogs for the rest of my life. I was totally in awe of them. The way they interact with us, their intelligence and sheer determination to integrate into our lives make them in my mind the most incredible and fascinating species of all. I even loved the dogs that weren't so nice.

One of these was my brother Richard's own dog, whose

name was Sally. She was a tall, slim, wire-haired lurcher, the colour of a custard cream. This particular lurcher was a result of crossing a collie x greyhound with a deerhound x saluki, which resulted in a nice-looking, super-athletic canine. She was very smart and clever from the collie side of the cross-breeding, had excellent hunting skills with sharp sight from the deerhound and saluki genes, and could race with the speed of lightning, which came from the greyhound side. So all these breeds carefully put together produced Sally.

This was no ordinary dog. No, Sally was incredibly reserved, with eyes of fire, and you could almost hear the cogs in her brain turning with intellect. She was a one-man dog, a hundred per cent devoted to Richard's every word and movement and part of his soul. They connected on such a level that everyone in our town of Bedworth knew who they were. One would hardly ever be without the other. They were always together, no matter what.

But whilst Sally was the perfect dog for Richard and never put a step wrong with him, she was the devil dog to our family. I laugh now, thinking back to her, but she really was such a difficult dog to live with. Her type of behaviour just would not be tolerated in this day and age. You could say she had a split personality. This perfectly behaved dog turned into a raving lunatic when my brother was out without her (which wasn't very often, thankfully). She had a very vicious side to her nature, and she hated being told what to do by anyone other than Richard. She could rule the house, and the fact she detested children really wasn't ideal either. I was around eight years old at the time, which was her perfect age for child hating!

My best friend Marcia and I would often want to go up to my bedroom to play with my dolls and doll's houses, but to get there we had to pass the old kitchen table, which was positioned about two feet away from the base of the stairs. The combination of the bottom three steps being missing from the staircase due to my dad's DIY, which was an ongoing thing in our house, and the fact the wicked troll (Sally) lived under the table when Richard was out made a recipe for disaster for us children.

Sure enough, Richard had gone out this particular afternoon and we wished to head upstairs to play. I called for my mum to move Sally from under the table.

'Mum, can you take Sally away so Marcia and I can play in my bedroom?'

My mum looked at Sally and instantly made eye contact. Marcia and I giggled as we saw Sally stare right back at my mum as if pre-empting what she was about to do. With a very slow controlled lift of her right lip, Sally showed my mum her large, sharp, glorious teeth, and with just as much control rolled her lip back down. It was a deliberate move-ment, done with style and poise.

'Well, girls,' my mum said, backing away whilst grinning to us, 'I'm not moving her. You'll need to wait until Richard comes back.' And she headed back to the sofa to read her paper.

Marcia and I looked at each other.

'You go first,' I said, pointing to the missing steps. 'But you'll have to take a run and jump and be quick.'

'Not on your nelly – she'll get me!' Marcia laughed.

'Go on! I'll try and distract her. Just run as fast as you can and then jump. By the time she moves to get you, you'll be up and on the fourth step safe, I promise. I'll be right behind you,' I chirped, confident Marcia would be able to outrun Sally.

'Right – are you ready?' I asked Marcia. I could see Sally with her head resting on her paws in front of her. She had her eyes locked like a missile on its target, her target on this occasion being us. Sally lay still, watching in silence. There was no emotion and no action. She was just watching and waiting for her prey. Well, that's what it felt like anyway.

Marcia straightened her top and took a deep breath, preparing herself for the leap of faith to that fourth step.

'Sally, stay!' I commanded, in my best Barbara Woodhouse tone of voice, but I swear I saw a slight curl of her lip as the words came out of my mouth. 'Ready? On the count of three. One, two . . .'

'Wait! I can't do it, she'll eat me!' Marcia was in fits of giggles whilst Sally looked on with that cold stare that could freeze the sun.

'Well, if you want to play with my new doll's house you'll need too. There's no other way.' And with that I gave her an unexpected push towards the stairs.

'Aghhh' was all I heard as poor Marcia flew screaming through the air between Sally and the step. Now, readers, I do realise this is no way to treat a best friend, but my intentions were good. I thought that with a little help she would get there faster (and I pushed her in the nicest possible way, of course, as only a good friend can).

There was certainly no going back at this point. As I watched Marcia throwing herself further than anticipated with the help of both my hands on her back, I could also see that custard cream-coloured devil dog launching herself towards Marcia's ankles with a look of determination and a mouth open, ready to bite.

'Helppp!' Marcia giggled as she landed on all fours on the fourth and sixth steps, narrowly escaping Sally's teeth, which were now thankfully retreating back under the table with the mouth they belonged to. It was a bit like a crocodile lying in wait just under the water at a watering hole as a zebra takes a well-earned drink. Then – wham! – the crocodile throws its whole body out of the water with a snap of its jaws to grab its prey, only to miss by inches and slowly slip back under the water, awaiting its next opportunity to attack. Yes, that was very much like Sally.

'Phew, oh my gosh! That was a close one,' Marcia panted with a sigh of relief.

'Joanne? What are you two up to? I hope you are not annoying Sally,' my mum called through, after hearing a thump as Marcia crash-landed onto the stairs.

'No, we are just playing. We are fine,' I replied, putting one finger up to my mouth to silence Marcia. 'Shhh, keep quiet!' I whispered, giggling.

'Now watch me – this is how you do it. I'm an expert at dodging the beast under the table,' I said, and took a couple of steps backwards so as to build up enough speed to fly past Sally and her amazingly white teeth.

'Here I go . . .' I called out as Marcia held her breath.

'Whooooooo . . .' I leapt as high as I could, but I hadn't realised that by leaping high I would not be able to jump far enough to reach the fourth step.

Snap snap went Sally's teeth. 'Aghhh,' I screamed, as I felt the wind whisk past my ankles, but somehow Marcia caught my hand and, with one sharp tug, pulled me to safety.

'Crikey, that was a close one,' Marcia laughed uncontrollably. 'I thought you said you were an expert?'

'So did I!' And we rolled about laughing, not even considering how we would attempt getting back down later.

Yes, Sally hated us children, in her unique, very self-controlled manner, and we did find it extremely funny at the time. Looking back, however, I should add that we were playing with fire. It was pretty irresponsible to have a dog which behaved in such a way around children or adults, but as a family we ignored her behaviour and just put it down to her being a grumpy old dog.

And back then we wouldn't have known how to correct the behaviour anyway. Most people didn't understand dog behaviour as we do today. As a nation we have come so far in understanding how dogs adapt to situations and to the expectations and guidelines of their owners. If Sally were living today, I have no doubt whatsoever that she would never have been allowed to create or sustain the aggression she had within her. We as a family or I as a communicator would have used techniques to imprint good behaviour from a young age and so enable her to live a harmonious life with those around her.

Marcia's family also kept dogs when I was growing up. They were lucky enough to have pure-bred golden Labradors. When Marcia and I were no older than seven, they owned a lovely dog called Sally. She may have had the same name as my brother Richard's lurcher, but she was very, very different in temperament. And she is the one I remember best.

This dog ate for England! She was shaped like a barrel, with a happy-go-lucky attitude. Everyone liked her. She was part of a very happy family and it showed. Non-stop wagging of her tail was a good indication. Her tail was enormous, and it used to spin so hard and fast that she might have taken off if she hadn't been so fat! It would start to wag in an up and down motion, then suddenly go round and round, making a huge circle of wind. And I am sure I saw her smile, too, her mouth quivering and lips curling – not in aggression but just because she was enjoying the pure thrill of us children playing and laughing as we did.

Many summer days were spent in the garden with Marcia, their other dog, Cindy, and the gorgeous Sally. We would spend hours playing find the bone, digging holes and hiding it between Marcia's dad's sweet pea canes. It was always fun and the dogs loved to join in our games. And when it was raining we played indoors, pretending the two dogs were ponies. They would happily oblige as we led them around the paddock (the living room) and pretended to place them into their stalls (between the sofas). We spent hours playing with them, but their ability to entertain us and stay enthusiastic never wavered.

One afternoon it was raining heavily. Outdoor play was a no go, so we decided to make a cake – a Victoria sponge, to be exact. We made our cake mixture with the help of Marcia's sister Nina. It was gloopy and tasted delicious. As both of us licked the spoons clean, Sally and Cindy, the two fat Labradors, sat looking on, longing for a taste.

'No, no, no,' we kept saying to them, laughing and giggling, but their huge brown eyes never left ours, eagerly awaiting any drop or spill of the mixture. Marcia, keen to be first, carefully spooned her mixture into her cake tin, which we had decided was going to form the bottom layer of our Victoria sponge. Then, very slowly, she walked over to the oven, holding the cake tin as if she was carrying the crown jewels, and placed it on the wire rack inside the warming oven.

Now it was my turn. I had the top layer, and for me this was the most important one of all. So, after expertly spooning it into the cake tin, making sure it was perfectly level and ready to bake into the perfect Victoria sponge top, I proceeded to walk to the oven. Within seconds the greased tin slid through my little fingers, which were already slippery with a mixture of cake and melted butter.

In slow motion, Cindy and Sally licked their lips and jumped up to catch the mixture, which was flying through the air from my hands and smack bang into the dogs' mouths!

We were all horrified to see my cake tin upside down on the floor with two very greedy Labradors attached to it, licking up every last drop of mixture, tails wagging hard in excitement. At least there was no mess left. They cleared every last drop off the floor and the cake tin looked like it had just come out of a dishwasher.

We had a very flat cake that day, splitting Marcia's single cake bottom into two and filling it with cream and jam. We ate slices of the cake with a bottle from the pop man (this was a local guy who drove a van clanking with bottles of fizzy drinks we called pop). And Cindy and Sally lay snoring loudly in the corner of the room, content with the delicacy of the cake mixture they had so eagerly devoured.

Nowadays when I have Labradors in my Animal Communication workshops, they remind me of those happy days as a child. Marcia and I are still in contact through Facebook and we often giggle together, sharing memories of the dogs.

I had one of my early sixth-sense experiences when I was just a young girl. It happened on a lazy summer afternoon when I was playing at a local place called the nook. This was just a few fields with a large pond with some swans on it. All the children in our area used to spend hours and hours there.

On this particular day I was happily playing in the grass collecting daisies when I noticed dark eyes staring at me through the bushes. I stopped what I was doing and stared right back.

'Hello,' I whispered.

And to my amazement the eyes blinked back at me.

'Do you need help?' I enquired, standing perfectly still. I wasn't scared at all. I just remember feeling it was my duty to help this dark-eyed soul. I knew in my heart he was not a threat to me. No, this animal needed comfort.

'Come, come here.' I waved my hands, coaxing him towards me. I wasn't very old at this point and so not tall, but I still felt the need to lower myself to his body level to help him feel relaxed. I knelt down slowly, to let those dark eyes know that I was here to help and was not a threat to him.

I recall sitting for about five minutes until, very slowly, a black Labrador-type dog crept out of the bushes. He was worried, but he bravely walked into my arms. In an instant our energy connected and he was wagging his tail in delight at finding a new friend.

I remember quite clearly knowing he was lost. I do not know how I knew this, but I never questioned my thought. As a child, you just don't. I knew he was on his own and lost. My instinct was to find a piece of rope and try and find his home.

I searched around, with the dog closely following behind, not leaving my side, until I found an old rope which had been tied around a fence post. I tied it loosely around his neck, and this black dog and I began to head home.

I kept asking him a very simple question: 'Which direction should we go?'

The dog pointed his wet nose in the air and I followed. But that wasn't all I did. In my head, I was saying to myself, Show me where to take him. At the time, I had no knowledge of spirit guides, but I must have been aware of an inner knowing or a guide of some description. Children often do have this awareness. They are more open than adults to the possibilities of another realm.

After about four miles, we were standing outside a block of grey flats. This is it, I said in my head.

Without warning, a lady with a purple scarf came running out of a blue door on the ground floor. And to my surprise I was met with, 'How dare you! That is my dog! You stole my dog!'

Before I could say anything, she snatched the rope out of my hand and went back into the flat with the dog, slamming the blue door behind her. I was left standing in shock, with my mouth open. There was no 'thank you for finding my dog', just abuse. But I was pleased that at least the dog had got home.

Looking back at this incident today, I realise I was communicating telepathically with the dog whilst also using my intuition. Even at such an early age, my sixth sense worked well. My intuition was taking me on a path of spiritual growth.

I had many psychic feelings and experiences when I was growing up, but I was too young and naive to understand what a gift I had. Yes, these experiences were remarkable and odd, but I couldn't explain them and, as yet, I didn't know how I could use the information I received.

I still had a lot to learn about the world of dogs and the different ways we allow them into our lives, be it as part of the family, as guard dogs or even as working dogs. We all have different relationships with them. Most are good, but sadly some are not.

I remember clearly an incident that took place at around this time, when I was still very young. I was playing with two other friends, Lara and Jenny, in the playing field behind our school. The large grass area was surrounded by beautiful oak trees that were always full of chirping birds and squirrels ready to entertain us by racing as fast as they could up and down the tree trunks, twitching their little noses and tails as if to catch our attention. Lara and Jenny were both animal lovers and we often played there. It always felt like a magical place to be because of all the interesting animals that played around us. We would also meet lots of different types of dogs, out with their owners taking an afternoon stroll, and we all enjoyed the excitement of getting to stroke or pat the dogs.

My friends and I had been playing in the field for several hours on this particular day. We were enjoying our school holidays, laughing and playing horses, with our skipping ropes wrapped around our waists for the other one to hold and shout 'Trot on!' It had been a lovely day and we were just about to leave for home when we noticed a tall, shadowy figure in the trees. We had a feeling that something wasn't right.

It was getting late, and all but one of the dog walkers and their dogs had headed back home for dinner. We were young and pretty scared. It was not normal to have strangers skulking about. In fact, nearly everyone in our small town knew everyone else. But we did the right thing and told the last dog walker about this strange figure we could see almost hidden within the trees, looking suspicious.

I began to feel quite sick and noticed a tingling in my arms, hands and fingers. At that time I didn't understand what was happening to me or know why I was feeling this way. That only became clearer later, when I was older, and I began to notice and recognise the warning signs of my gift of communication. For now, I was just pleased that the gentleman dog walker proceeded to go and investigate further. He was probably thinking that the stranger might be waiting around to harm children like ourselves who were just out playing.

We followed cautiously across the field, a few steps behind the gentleman and his big hairy German shepherd dog, fondly known to us as Butch. He was a huge dog, with a massive black shiny nose and enormous white teeth, which could look quite scary, yet he was so very gentle, and loved meeting us children for a good cuddle and kiss.

Butch began to bark as we approached the edge of the woods and we all saw someone dark-haired running away as fast as he could. He was a teenager of around fourteen or fifteen years of age. Butch was now barking ferociously at him, whilst we children huddled together, shaking in terror of what might lie ahead. The teenager ran at high speed through and over the fallen branches and logs, heading directly out of the opposite side of the woods. The dog walker was calling after him, 'Oi, you boy, come back! What have you done?'

What I saw next is something I have, up until now, put absolutely to the back of my mind. It was a beautiful, silvery blue-coloured greyhound hanging by a thin, tatty, cream-coloured rope. The rope had been tied firmly around her neck and attached directly to a large tree branch. The dog just hung like a lead weight before our tear-filled eyes. All her breath and fight had gone and she was indeed dead.

I tried to look away, as the horror of what I saw in front of me was quickly embedding itself deep into my mind, but I couldn't help myself from staring at her and feeling the trauma and pain. The suffering was unbearable. What this poor innocent dog had gone through must have been utterly horrific, yet we had heard nothing. And the reason soon became apparent. The stranger had taped her mouth tightly closed with wrappings of thick black tape. Whatever noise or struggle she may have made, we certainly wouldn't have heard her cries for help.

It was terrible. I felt so guilty, so sad and utterly useless. How could anyone have done this to a dog? I began to realise that all the sickness and the tingling feelings had gone. Now I just felt numb, heartbroken and empty. Perhaps this was how she had felt before she died? Perhaps I had experienced a connection to her and hadn't realised. I will never know.

I haven't spoken about this until now. It hurts every time I relive that day. That image, that scene is imprinted in my mind. It taught me, when I was only little, that not everyone in this world feels like me about animals. To some people, a dog may be a scavenging mutt, something to abuse, something to throw out when not needed, something that feels nothing, has no emotions and no rights. It has no life of its own because 'it's just a dog'.

Nowadays I feel my gift as an Animal Communicator comes with a responsibility to share my knowledge. I try to help people understand that dogs think and feel, love and grieve, feel pain and loss just as we humans do. They may not be human, but they are living, breathing, sentient beings. I think of them as our very own angels with fur, cleverly disguised, with those adorable eyes filled with unconditional love, shiny wet noses and waggy tails that melt your heart!

And the most amazing revelation is that these dogs and puppies, from every walk of life, every type, shape or size, whether pedigree or cross-breed, can all communicate easily with humans on a deep, interesting and often surprising level. They know far more than we ever give them credit for, and they can tell you the truth about how they really feel and what they need to live a happy and contented life.

Throughout my life I have had the ability to connect with my own dogs through a psychic, telepathic, intuitive link, and with none more so than my beautiful late borzoi Mozart.

Mozart was a tall, stunning, mahogany and white-coloured boy, with the longest of noses and the kindest, most soulful eyes I have ever seen. He was so very special and he touched my heart like no other dog I have ever had the pleasure of sharing my life with. I am not suggesting I loved him any more or less than the others. I am saying he was different. Somewhere deep inside my heart lay a place that only he and I shared, somewhere I don't think I will share with any other. He was my dream borzoi and I miss him dearly.

I had actually purchased him as a two-year-old for showing and he became my teacher at dog shows. He taught me everything I needed to know about handling dogs in the ring and showing them to their best. He gave me the skills I needed to present the winning borzoi. And when I had learnt all that he had to teach me, he decided that was it.

One day at a local championship show I pulled up into the parking area just behind the trade stands, which were by now being swamped by eager exhibitors buying the last few essentials such as number holders and grooming spray before going into the ring with their dogs. I turned off the car engine and turned to look at Mozart, who was stretched out on the back seat on his blanket. His communication with me was emotional rather than through the spoken words that I hear in most readings. Mozart would make me feel what he was thinking.

On this occasion I knew in my heart that he didn't want to get out of the car. I felt an incredible ache. In my mind, the answer no came shooting right back at me, as if I had already asked the question, Are you coming?

I decided to go round to the door anyway, open it and invite him to follow me. Mozart lifted his head and looked me straight in the eye before lifting his body up into a sitting position. That look said a thousand words to me. It told me he wasn't coming, he had finished. Mozart was done. His days of showing were over.

My heart ached with sadness that we were not going to show again. He had been such an amazing teacher and a great dog to show. I loved turning heads as we glided around the ring together in unison. Everyone could see how absolutely gorgeous he was, with his long coat blowing in the wind like some majestic creature from another world. But how could I force such a dog to do something he no longer wished to do? I couldn't. I leant into the car, gave him a huge kiss on his long nose, closed the door and headed home. That was the last time Mozart and I ever went to a dog show together.

By listening to your heart, you will always hear the truth. Some would call it gut instinct. If you feel it, take notice and react. That way you will know you have always done the right thing by your animal and will have no guilt, no regret, ever. For me Mozart's truth came through his heart. He made me aware of what he needed through that strange thing we call love. And you too can have this with your own dogs.

Chapter Two

In my opinion, dogs have the closest bond with humans of all animals. They seem to have a unique way of interacting with us, and a special ability to connect on a deep emotional level. They burn their love into the hearts of even the most cold-hearted people. When we feel the love of a dog, we cannot help loving them back. Those big eyes, that wet black nose and the wagging tail are all irresistible.

I never cease to be amazed at the relationship we develop with dogs. Through my workshops, I see so many cases of pure love and true connection that it melts me. The heroic dogs, the jesters, the companions all have a job to do and I believe they help us humans understand what love is. My role is to further the connection, so that people are able to get the most out of their relationship with their puppies and dogs.

I first met Wesley around four years ago, at my friend Claire's house. I had arrived at about seven o'clock and was enjoying a few pre-dinner drinks when a very smart-looking dog with huge floppy ears and a beard wandered into the living room.

Wesley wasn't a pure-bred dog but a labradoodle, which is a cross between a Labrador and a poodle. So along with the Labrador mix he had a gorgeous black curly coat, which had obviously come from the poodle side, and the most handsome, wise face. And he was huge. He was a cross with the largest of the three sizes of poodle, which we call a standard, and he was about the size of a small pony. As Claire didn't have a dog I was a little surprised to see him.

'Ah, you two have met, then?' Claire said as she walked into the room.

'Well, yes – but whose is he?' I asked, smiling, as I encouraged him towards me for a stroke.

'Long story,' Claire laughed.

'So, go on – tell me,' I said, interested.

'Well, you remember Duncan, my ex?' she began.

'Oh, yes! "Duncan the delightful". Not the best choice you have made,' I giggled.

'Joanne! That's not fair, he was lovely – sort of . . .' she laughed.

'Oh, Claire – you dumped him because he was boring and you couldn't have a conversation without falling asleep,' I teased. 'So it's his dog, then? What's his name?'

'His name is Wesley, and no, it's not his dog. Well, not really,' she replied.

'So whose is he, then?' I asked, now rubbing Wesley's ears, to his delight.

'Well, he's his ex-wife's ex-boyfriend's mother's dog,' she said, trying to work it out.

'Now I'm confused. But why do you have him?' I asked.

'Oh, well, the mother unfortunately died and left the dog to the son. He is not a dog lover so the girlfriend took him (that's Duncan's ex-wife). But then she got a job abroad and so Duncan took him from her. Now Duncan has a job for two weeks in the north of Scotland and I said I'd look after him for him. And to be honest, I'm not sure what I'm supposed to do. I don't really like dogs, and he isn't exactly Lassie, is he? But I felt bad for Duncan after dumping him. I thought it would make him feel better. You know how devastated he was,' she said, looking a little guilty.

'Well, I think it's great. It's about time you had a new man in your life, isn't it, Wesley?' I said, ruffling his neck and ears.

'But I think he is odd. All he does is sleep. And he snores. It's worse than having a man!' she said.

'Do you, Wesley? Are you a sleepy dog? I'm not surprised. Claire's boring too, just like your daddy, eh?' I said teasingly.

'Thanks a bunch,' she laughed, handing me another drink.

'He just doesn't do it for me. You know me, Joanne, I'm not a dog lover at all, and he just sleeps, snores loudly and smells. What should I do?'

'Give me some peace,' a deep husky voice piped up.

Now this was not my voice, nor was it Claire's. And the only other person, or should I say dog, in the room was the handsome Wesley.

I looked at Claire and laughed. 'Give him some peace, he has just said.'

'What? Are you chatting to dogs again, Joanne? Do you ever stop? Anyway, you would say that. You'd be on his side,' Claire said, not believing my message.

This was not a surprise, as she wasn't an animal lover. And she was a full-blown sceptic. I have found this is quite normal for people who have no connection with animals. They see them as animals and nothing more. And let's face it, Claire only had Wesley through guilt from dumping Duncan and not because she actually wanted a dog.

'Claire, he is a talking, walking, gorgeous dog with feelings, you know!' I laughed. 'You wait and see.'

'Umm. So why does he sleep so much? Is there something wrong with him?' she asked.

'There's nothing wrong with me. What does she want

me to do – bounce around the house all day?' Wesley replied quite sarcastically.

'Why is he looking at me that way? Tell him to stop!' she winced, pulling a face of disapproval.

Actually, I nearly choked on my drink as I saw Wesley staring at her with utter disgust and Claire looking back at him side on, with her bottom lip stretching down at the sight of the dog giving her the eye.

'Ooh, he's weird,' she snapped.

'Tell her she's weird!' he snapped back.

'Look, he's got the eyes of a gremlin.'

'Tell her she has the eyes of a . . .'

'Stop!' I laughed. 'You two are as bad as each other. Why can't you just get on?'

'Why? What's he been saying?' Claire wondered.

'It doesn't matter what he has been saying. It's about what you are saying. He hears every word, and you are being disrespectful to him,' I replied.

'It's a dog, Joanne, just a dog,' Claire said.

'And she's just a stupid human!' he replied.

'Look, you are human, Claire,' (I left out the stupid bit) 'and you,' I said, looking at Wesley, 'are a very handsome dog. So let's all get on and enjoy our night.'

I couldn't believe that I was in the middle of an argument between a dog and my friend, and I couldn't help but wonder how on earth these two were ever going to get along.

Claire got up and walked into the kitchen, mumbling under her breath about having to look after him.

'Claire, is there no one else who could have taken Wesley?' I called through to her.

'I've no idea. Duncan asked me and I felt obliged, really. Stupid, I know, but I felt I should,' she replied.

'Hey, I am here, you know,' Wesley said, walking past me and heading to the square brown bed in the corner of the room.

Now labradoodles are smart, and Wesley was no exception.

'Claire, you know how clever this dog is. You two could really have a good relationship if you tried,' I said, hoping she would listen.

'Well, I'm not looking for a relationship. I just want to get the time with him over and done with and then he can go back to where he came from, and the sooner the better,' Claire said.

'Wow! Such a caring human! Does she not know I don't like her either'? Wesley said.

It was like a sparring match, back and forth. I couldn't believe a dog and human could live side by side with such animosity between them. How on earth was I going to heal the rift between these two?

Claire put the food on the table. It was a lovely lasagne and jacket potatoes, and as I sat down, pulling my chair up to the table ready to feast, I said, 'Claire, this looks delicious! You shouldn't have gone to so much trouble.'

'She didn't. It's out of a box. I saw it,' Wesley said sarcastically, sniffing the air. 'My mum always let me lick the boxes. She doesn't. She's mean.'

I couldn't help but giggle at Wesley's comment. I know my dog Rosie loves to finish off my leftover food.

After dinner, I suggested we all go for a walk around the local park to burn off some calories.

'Does he have to come?' Claire asked, pointing at Wesley.

'Yes, and he is right, you know!' I laughed.

'What about?' Claire looked puzzled.

'You. You are mean!' I said, giggling at Claire as she stomped to the back door to put on her shoes.

'Blumming dog,' she mumbled.

'Come on, Wesley. Let's go, there's a good boy,' I called to him as he came over, looking pleased with himself for having annoyed her some more. He certainly wasn't bothered by Claire's lack of love. It just made him enjoy winding her up even more.

We had walked for about half a mile when we met a few other people with their dogs. I made Claire hold Wesley's lead so that she got used to having him with her. It was a strange sight, seeing Claire walking a dog. She is normally too clean and well turned out to walk a dog, and she was wearing heels, as usual, because she always likes to look her best.

Wesley strolled on with Claire and myself in tow. All of a sudden a squirrel ran out from the left-hand side and shot straight across the path we were on and up the tree on the right, closely followed by Wesley. He went bounding after the squirrel and attached securely to his lead was Claire.

I gasped as I saw her fly towards the tree, unable to let go as her hand was through the loop of the lead.

'My shoes!' she screamed, as she skipped across the muddy grass at full speed after Wesley. Of course by this time I was in fits of laughter, seeing her frantically trying to stay upright. I couldn't move for laughing. It was hysterical!

'Hold on, Claire. He'll stop soon,' I shouted, almost choking on my laughter.

'Aghhhh' came the scream.

Oh, my gosh, she was down. Wesley had actually pulled her down, slap bang in the mud. Forget getting her shoes dirty – her whole body was dirty now. She was covered in mud!

'I'm going to kill him,' she screamed at Wesley, as I put out my hand to pick her up, tears of laughter rolling down my face.

'That's dogs for you,' I laughed.

'What's she doing on the ground?' Wesley said, turning to see what all the fuss was about.

I explained to him that he had pulled her over when he ran after the squirrel. To my surprise he immediately walked straight up to her and licked and nuzzled her hand with affection.

And at that moment, the connection appeared. Claire looked down at Wesley, who was now looking up at her with huge puppy eyes that not even Claire could resist, and, brushing herself off, she gave him a little pat on the head. It was not quite a stroke, but a pat at least. She said, 'Oh, they were old shoes. Anyhow, I suppose I'm going to have to get used to it, eh?'

I was amazed. Just five minutes ago Claire and Wesley were enemies, and now? Well, it seemed they might be friends. What had happened?

Well, I will tell you. The love of Wesley's heart is what happened. He felt sorry for her and gave her a chance of connection. And she couldn't resist. Very few can, in fact. When a dog or puppy offers up its love, it is very hard to refuse.

Sadly, Wesley himself is no longer with us but the memory of that day will stay with me for ever. We often laugh about the memories of Claire having to walk home covered in mud.

The gorgeous Wesley actually ended up living with Claire full-time. He became a really close friend and a dog she will never forget. So you see, even non-doggy people can be touched by love at some point in their lives. I know Claire was.

I've seen so many people and their pooches over the years in my work as a communicator, and one thing that always strikes me is the similarities between the owners and their loved dogs. Many owners simply act as their dogs do and vice versa. They share the same type of personality, and the same way of talking. Owners who have tempers often have dogs with bad tempers, or they may be really chatty and so too are their dogs. And quite often they even look the same.

Mentioning no names so as not to shame them, I have a female friend who has long golden blonde hair. Her beautiful dog is a stunning golden Afghan and I swear they look just the same from the back. Not only that but they walk in a similar way, with an elegant stride. And their personalities are remarkably alike. My friend is quite snooty (in a nice way) – she only likes the people she knows and is quite aloof with strangers – and so is her dog!

Another gentleman I know is the spitting image of his dog. The two of them look so much like each other it's scary.

They both have huge grey beards, exactly the same shape and the same salt and pepper colour. And they are both profoundly stubborn and self-reliant.

There is nothing better than seeing people who look like their dogs. It always makes me laugh but it comes as no surprise. When they are really connected, dogs and owners tend to morph into each other, much as husbands and wives do. Have a look at the people you know with dogs. Trust me, if it's not yourself (be honest), there will be someone you know who is identical to their dog.

Many years ago, when I first started working professionally as an Animal Communicator, I visited a friend called Libby. She had been having several problems with her little puppy, Tyson.

Tyson was purchased on a whim. Libby wasn't looking for a dog at the time. In fact, it had been the last thing on her mind. She had never wanted another dog after the trauma of losing her childhood pet. Now, thirty years on, her life seemed just fine without one.

Then one day, after doing her shopping at the local market, Libby noticed a man standing in the small car park where she had left her car. He began signalling and waving at her to come over to his van. She did not know the man and any normal person would have walked in the other direction, but not Libby. She wondered what he wanted. Why would he be waving at her? He seemed keen to show her what he had in his van with the blacked-out windows, and she could hear faint whimpers coming from the open doors. The little whimpers were not of the human kind and they warmed her heart before she could even work out what they were.

As Libby approached the van, she could see a spade, two shovels, a few old rags and a bag of cement in the back. Between these items was a small rusty wire cage, about the size of a large crisp box, which had been bedded with old newspaper, torn to tiny shreds. The paper was almost obscuring the little wet noses of some puppies, who were fighting to be heard and seen by passers-by. There were four in total, climbing on top of each other and pushing tiny padded paws down onto the other heads to gain pole position. One was a shade of blue, one the colour of a tiger and the other two a creamy beige, like the magnolia paint that was so popular in homes throughout the 1990s. But Libby's eyes were fixed on the little blue puppy and his eyes were fixed right back. He was staring at her with a pleading face that not even the hardest criminal could have resisted.

'Twenty quid. You can take one away now, twenty quid only. Just what your son or daughter wants,' said the guy whilst scanning the car park like a radar, searching for the police. In the back of her mind Libby worried slightly that she too would be prosecuted if the police did catch them trading. Was it even legal? But that little blue puppy kept her heart and mind focused on him.

'Umm, I don't have children,' Libby replied.

'Well, he doesn't have a mum. Poor little fellow, he is,' he said, pointing to the blue puppy that he could see Libby staring at through the wires of the cage. 'The perfect match, don't you think? He needs a mum just like you, that he does.' And as quick as you like he reached into the cage and whisked the puppy into Libby's arms.

She stared down to see the little pup licking his lips and stretching his neck as far as he could manage, just to reach her face for a kiss. His little tail was wagging so hard it constantly whipped Libby's side. He was only about the size of a rolled-up ball of socks – minus the legs, head and tail, that is. He struggled a little, but this tiny little blue bundle of smelly puppy breath had found his way into Libby's heart. At the same time he had successfully managed to wiggle his way up to her face and was now lapping at Libby's cold nose, eager for approval and attention.

Libby panicked at her utter helplessness. She had fallen in love instantly, but she also noticed a disgusted look from a passer-by who was tutting to himself. She quickly placed the puppy back into the arms of the man before she had the chance to do something silly, like buy him.

'I'm sorry. I can't. I don't have twenty pounds on me. I've just been shopping and only have a ten pound note,' she said. This was a lie, as she actually had around fifty pounds after visiting the cashpoint, but she was hoping this would put the man off. She smiled politely, gave the puppy one last look goodbye, picked up her bag and started to walk back to her car.

'Lady, wait,' the man called as he tapped her arm. 'A tenner it is.' And he thrust the pup back into her arms. 'If you don't take him today, well, they will all have to be drowned. I can't take them back. The wife won't have it.' He gave her a pleading look.

Libby looked down at the puppy, which began wagging his little tail with delight at being in her arms once more. And again, her heart melted into a mush of love.

'Drowned? Really? That's awful – why?' she asked worriedly.

'Wife hates dogs. She told me they had to go, today, and not to come back with the blighters. Their own mum died two days ago and she said they must go too. She said if I brought them back she would drown them, which she would, let me assure you. She's a hard, cold-hearted woman. Not like you,' he smiled. 'So I thought I'd try one last chance and sell them here. I'll take that tenner then, deal?' He winked.

Libby wasn't sure whether he was telling the truth or spinning her a line. She felt the latter was probably the truth of the matter and she knew it was wrong to buy anything dodgy, let alone live puppies out of a van in a car park. But she couldn't take the chance. She needed to do something.

'OK, I will take all four at ten pounds each, take it or leave it. They will come with me now, but I will need that cage as I don't have anything to put them in.'

She put her hand into her purse as the pup wiggled his body closer into her chest and pulled out four crisp ten-pound notes. Placing the cage with the four puppies safely onto the back seat of her car, Libby handed the money over.

'Thank you, lovely lady. You won't regret it!' The man walked away, grinning to himself and shuffling the four notes through his fingers in delight.

Libby got herself into the car, closed and locked the door and turned her head around to see what she had done. There, staring back, were the little rolled-up socks, with wet noses, streaming eyes and breath that was a combination of sweaty armpits and the finest Belgian chocolate. Libby could not believe what she had purchased. What on earth was she going to do with one puppy, let alone four?

Taking a deep breath to calm herself down, she decided to drive to the local dog shelter. Luckily Libby had been to school with the centre manager and had known her and her family for years, so she was sure the centre would help her in whatever way they could.

The staff at the dog shelter took one look at the puppies and shook their heads. 'Where exactly did you get them?' the centre manager asked, as she peered into the cage. Libby told her what had happened and how she just couldn't leave them to be drowned.

'That old story! It's quite common, Libby. You know that, don't you? You were duped, I'm afraid. It's the oldest trick in the book. Pull at someone's heartstrings and you have yourself a sale,' the centre manager said, shaking her head in disgust. 'They don't look well to me. We will have the vet look at them immediately. Would you like to stay and see what the vet has to say, Libby?'

Libby nodded, feeling responsible for the puppies, and took a seat in the waiting room whilst the puppies were hurried off to the vet's office for closer inspection.

It seemed forever before the centre manager came out of the vet's room, her face looking somewhat sad. Libby wondered what was wrong as she stood to receive the news.

'You did indeed save them, Libby. In fact, if you hadn't

got them when you did they would have died an agonising death,' the centre manager began.

'What do you mean? Are they OK?' Libby felt confused.

'Well, they are really poorly. They have what's called parvovirus.* This can be passed down from the mother . . .'

'She's dead,' Libby butted in. 'Just two days ago, apparently.'

'Well, I don't hold out much hope for these little ones either. They are very ill, but we will do all we can. We will keep them under strict observation and treatment and see what happens. It's in the lap of the gods, I'm afraid. It may be a few days before we know whether any of them will pull through.'

*The disease canine parvovirus is highly contagious and is normally spread from dog to dog by direct or indirect contact with their faeces. It can be especially severe in puppies that are not protected by maternal antibodies, like the puppies in Libby's case, or if puppies have not been vaccinated, something that we should all do when we bring a new dog into our home. Your vet can advise on a suitable vaccination routine.

Dogs that develop the parvovirus disease normally show symptoms of the illness within five to ten days. These include vomiting, lethargy, fever and severe diarrhoea (usually with blood). Severe vomiting and diarrhoea result in dehydration, and secondary infections will most probably set in. Dogs have a distinctive odour in the later stages of the infection. If the disease is not caught early enough, shock and then death are likely to occur in most cases.

Libby left the shelter in a state of shock. Her day had been just like any other until the meeting in the car park, but now it had turned upside down. That evening, she couldn't eat anything through worry. And when she tried to sleep, the picture of the little blue puppy that so eagerly wanted her attention kept coming into her mind. Even though he and his litter mates must have been feeling so poorly, they had still had the strength to plead for her love. Libby prayed that night for the first time in years, asking for the safe recovery of the pups.

A few days passed and the news from the shelter was good. All four puppies were doing well. The treatment was working and, whilst still in isolation, all four were going to make a full recovery. Libby was ecstatic! She couldn't help wondering about the blue pup and phoned every day for the following fortnight to see how he was doing.

'He's quite a character, isn't he?' the centre manager laughed. 'I take it you are going to keep this one, then? I think he'd be good for you, a bit of company. One of the vet nurses wants to adopt the two cream pups. And I'd quite like the little stripy one myself. Which leaves the naughty one for you. So, do you want him?' she asked, laughing.

'Oh, umm, yes, I suppose I could take him. He did seem to like me. It's been years since I had a dog, but I am sure it will be fine.'

A little time later all four puppies went to their new homes. The young vet nurse's hero was Bill Oddie, so the two cream ones were named Bill and Oddie. The centre manager took the stripy pup home and called him Sausage, for no other reason than she fed him sausages a lot whilst he was in her care.

Libby took home the naughtiest, funniest, happiest little puppy, the one that had picked her as his new human mum right at the beginning. Continually biting and nibbling his litter brothers' ears, he was known to everyone as Tyson, after the notorious ear-biting bad boy Mike Tyson. If I tell you he led her a merry dance, that would be an understatement. He drove her stir-crazy, not doing as he was told, constantly testing her authority, and creating all kinds of havoc.

He raided her rubbish bins during the night whilst she was sleeping, leaving a fabulous trail of rotting leftovers, from cabbage, yogurt pots and home-made lasagne to empty tins of tomato soup, carefully rolled along her beige carpet in colourful artistic splashes.

He would open her bedside drawers and pull out every item of underwear, new and old, chewing holes in each and every garment so that they looked like a little moth had been throwing the last dinner party for all the moths in the world.

No matter what she tried, he would not house-train, and

when she had guests over he would promptly position himself in full view of them and, with a look of happiness washing over his cute little stubby face, proceed to poop the largest, smelliest poop he could muster.

Yes, Tyson was a little monster!

Libby took him back to the vet for a check-up to make sure he wasn't deaf or suffering from some sort of mental disorder. But no, he turned out to be totally fine and healthy. The only conclusion was that he was just a little naughty and so, in the hope that a solution could be found, she called me in to try and help, through communication and possibly a little magic.

Now, I must point out that whilst it can sometimes seem that magic has occurred, this is something I don't know how to do – certainly not in the Paul Daniels and David Copperfield way. But my work can certainly be magical. I think of it as being like sitting in the sun on a long, hot, summer day. You don't understand how it works but you know the warmth is there and that it makes you feel good.

There is some sort of mystery to my work, and the mystery is noticeable to me as well. Even though I understand the process of communication between human and animal, my work and its results can still astonish me, knock me sideways, make me stand and gasp, 'Did that really just happen?' There are times when, in a way that is almost like magic, the animal listens to what I have to say, absorbs the information, and then has a magical transformation. So the word I like to use is magical and not magic when referring to Animal Communication.

When I first met Tyson he was certainly not showing magical transformation. No, he was showing determination to completely ignore Libby, me and anyone else who happened to be passing by. He wouldn't listen to anything Libby or I had to say. Instead he chose to parade around the living room with a pair of Libby's newly chewed red knickers and ignore us all. Boy, he was cute – very cute, in fact – and you couldn't help but fall in love with his podgy little body and short stubby face with legs to match. I couldn't work out what breed he was, although I suspect there was some Jack Russell somewhere in that body. But as he was even smaller than a normal-sized Jack Russell and a deep blue colour, he might have had a tiny chihuahua cross in there too.

At the time, dogs like this were seen as common crossbreeds, of no use to anyone, which is probably why the man couldn't get rid of them fast enough. In recent years, dogs like little Tyson have become highly sought after. Small, compact and very cute, with a diva attitude to match, he would now probably sell for around six hundred pounds to some young glamourpuss who wanted a small dog to carry around in her handbag as a fashion accessory. However, I can't help thinking that if Tyson was indeed in some lady's Prada or Gucci handbag he would rip out all the lining with his little teeth, eat all her money and chew the contents of her super swish bag with sheer delight! Thankfully, this pup was never meant to be one of those dogs. He was just him – naughty to the core and Libby's.

Nothing worked that day. I tried all the communication techniques I could think of, but it was like he had earplugs in, big fat silencing ones, capable of totally blocking out the world around him. Whether I spoke out loud to him or spoke quietly in my mind, trying to connect at a telepathic level, the information just wouldn't get through. I was exhausted, but I told Libby that, somehow, I would find a way of getting through to the little tyke.

It was only on my way home that I came up with a cunning plan, something that would indeed get his attention. I suppose you could call it a diversion. But it would take more than me to carry it out. I would have to call in backup in the form of another dog – an older, wiser and stricter dog. We humans couldn't get through, but perhaps another dog just might be able to. And so the next day we arranged for Cindy, a beautiful golden Labrador known to all in the neighbourhood as 'the dog with the brain', to come along.

Well, as you know, all dogs have brains but Cindy was

something else, something special. I had done a reading with her previously and she was so wise about life. She told me so much about her duties as a care dog and how it was her mission to help and care for those around her. It was her work, her need, her love.

She looked out for her human mum, her dad, her mum and dad's children, their children and so on. She stood quietly so that little old ladies who needed something to lean on could rest with one hand on her back whilst they took a few breaths before continuing on their journey. She helped toddlers stand up by letting them get hold of her tail and pull themselves off the floor, collected the morning newspapers from the grocery store on her own, and even once, when she was just a young pup herself, rescued three kittens that had been thrown in the local canal in a tied carrier bag by swimming in and retrieving them safely to shore. Yes, Cindy was the dog of all dogs to get through to Tyson. If she couldn't do it, I honestly didn't know who would.

So the plan was set. I was to ask Cindy to talk with Tyson and find out why he was naughty, why he wouldn't listen, and let him know he had to start to behave in an acceptable way.

Tyson took one look at Cindy, tail-wagging mischief in his eyes, and began attempting to climb all over her. Cindy moved slowly out of his way and he tried again. This happened at least five times but Cindy had the patience of a saint.

Then, on his next attempt, Cindy looked Tyson right in the eye and gave him a look that was not one of her 'Will you just stop it now, please' looks. It was more of the 'Stop, now!' variety, with an added slight curl of her top right-hand lip revealing one large super-white tooth. To our amazement, Tyson immediately plonked his little fat puppy bottom down on the floor, made a whimper noise and listened to her intently.

Libby and I looked at each other in silence, both knowing what was happening. He was absolutely transfixed by Cindy. He followed her around, copied what she did and behaved perfectly for the few hours she was there with him. Tyson was like the ideal puppy. He even went out for a poop and pee with her, copying her sniffing a certain patch of grass and then turning his back so as not to be seen by us humans, who were standing watching, in awe of this puppy trying so hard to be just like Cindy.

Later that evening I did a reading with Cindy and asked her what she thought of little Tyson. The outcome was simple. Cindy explained, 'He just needs showing what to do. His mum never taught him anything as she was too ill and he was too young when she left him. I showed him how to be a good dog, that's all.' The plan had worked!

It was that easy. He needed to learn from his own kind. Dogs normally show their babies what is right and wrong from the start, so they know how to behave. Only for Tyson this didn't happen. His mum was very ill and then eventually died, all before he was five weeks old, and he never did learn.

Libby took Tyson to meet Cindy for play and learning up until she passed away some years later, and with her lovely influence Tyson turned out to be a great dog for Libby. He was well behaved, good company and above all well loved (even if he was still a little partial to stealing Libby's sexiest underwear now and then and chewing out the gussets).

It took communication and the teachings of another dog to finally get through to him. My part, although small in this case, was to find a way of communicating with him. And that I accomplished. Saint Cindy's memory will always live on in Tyson for all who admire him as the small, slightly porky, stumpy-legged, thoroughly well-behaved dog he is today.

People often talk about angel pets and I find this a lovely turn of phrase. I do believe that all pets are in fact angels. Animals have this unique ability to help heal and soften our souls, which means that, in my mind, they are angelic and special. When I hear about the remarkable relationships that some of my clients have with their four-legged furry friends – the bonds, the trust, the incredible connection they have with each other – I wonder who could ever doubt that they are angels.

How many times have you seen your dog connect with you when you are feeling a little low? The dog has the capability to feel your emotions. Dogs know! Maybe they will put a head on your lap for comfort or there will be a quiet moment of understanding between you. Dogs have created a bond with us like no other animal.

A few years ago, I had the pleasure of meeting a guy called Henry and his dog, Angel. If ever a dog had the perfect name, it was this one.

Henry was a forty-something gentleman who was happily married with three children, living in Scotland, holding down a good job in IT and enjoying life to the full. His world was suddenly turned upside down after a freak car accident in which he suffered multiple fractures and injuries. These meant Henry was unable to work and he was signed off for many months to recover.

The healing process of his body slowly began, but Henry's mental health deteriorated. He withdrew from people around him and found it really hard to communicate or get back to life as it had been before the accident. Henry got so bad that he eventually lost his job, his house and finally his wife and children. He had changed so much from the husband and father they once knew that they found they couldn't live with him any more.

Within a year of the accident Henry had lost everything he had once held so dear. It was as if he had pushed his very own self-destruct button and was powerless to stop the down-hill slide. He was now homeless and living rough on the streets. Whatever money he managed to get from passers-by he spent on drink, often getting through two bottles of neat vodka in one day. Henry's dignity, well-being and health were now at rock bottom and so he made the decision to end his life, not even thinking how that might affect anyone else. The only person he could think about at this stage was himself.

But on the evening Henry was to end it all, his life changed in a way he could never have imagined. He walked up to the bridge from which he was planning to jump, but when he got there he saw a small brown cross-breed dog tied to the railings. She was all on her own, whimpering. He looked around for her owner but saw no one. He waited at least three hours, just in case someone came back for her, but nobody turned up. And in those hours Henry forgot why he was there himself. His original idea had left his mind because now his focus was purely on helping the abandoned dog.

Seeing she was a little distressed and on her own, he took her back to the place where he normally slept and the two of them became inseparable, keeping each other warm at night and being great company for each other during the day. Rather than spending any money he received on alcohol, Henry bought food, a coat and bedding for the little dog. He took more care of himself, too. Walking her through the park, he began noticing the flowers, birds and insects around him. His senses and awareness of the world started to return.

The two of them bonded so well that they made an impact on passers-by. Because of the dog, people would stop and talk, which they hadn't done before when Henry was on his own. The dog seemed to attract people and Henry would tell everyone the story of how she had saved his life. Henry began to communicate again, something he hadn't been able to do for so long.

Even though he was still living rough, Henry now had something to live for. He sought help through a homeless charity and within a few months he and the dog had found a shared home to live in. He managed to get a part-time job and life began to look bright again. Henry called the little dog Angel because she had clearly saved his life, for which he will be forever grateful.

Today, Henry is happy to report that his life is going great. He sees his children on a regular basis and has a good relationship with his ex-wife. Looking back, he finds it hard to believe how bad life actually got after the accident. The pair found each other just as Henry was on the brink of ending his own life. If it wasn't for finding Angel, he would most definitely have gone through with his suicide, with devastating effects for all his family.

And Henry's life turned another corner when he met his new partner, Liz. He is living with her in a new house and still sharing his life with Angel. Being able to overcome all obstacles together, no matter how difficult, means everything. Henry, Liz and Angel the dog can look forward to a bright future.

I thought you might enjoy reading Jennifer Quinn's story about her dog Monty, who has been a guardian angel to her.

Joanne, here is my story about my adorable little dog Monty.

I was born with a disability called spina bifida, which affects my mobility. I can walk with the aid of crutches, but mostly I am confined to a wheelchair. My disability made me very depressed, as I lived on my own before Monty came along and at times I felt so isolated and alone.

But June 1998 was one of the best months of my life. I was out shopping, just minding my own business, when I decided to have a look at the adverts in the shop windows and out jumped this one: 'West Highland white terriers looking for a loving home'. I had always wanted another dog since my last one had passed over nine years before and, although my first dog could never be replaced, I knew something was missing from my life. I knew in my heart that this advert was the answer.

So Monty, as I named him – after the film *The Full Monty* and Monty Magpie, the Newcastle United mascot – came to live with me. Monty is a small male dog with big brown friendly eyes and a soft black shiny nose. His hair is pure white, very thick and straight. He is the most laid-back dog I know, and not a lot fazes him, apart from stairs. He's a small bundle of fun, into everything, and had me absolutely worn out from day one. He never sleeps past 6 a.m. and though I've never been a morning person, he started work on me straightaway. This little dog may have had his work cut out, but he certainly wasn't going to just sit back and let me slip deeper into depression.

When I first started taking Monty for walks he used to pull me over in his eagerness to get out and explore. Being on crutches makes it nearly impossible for me to hold onto a lead with a dog that pulls, but we've learned the best way of doing things now and, although he wasn't too happy about it at first, I managed to get a head harness on him. His favourite thing to do is to go for walks, so it was great to reach a compromise so that we can both enjoy them. Monty doesn't play with anything, though! If you were to throw a ball he'd just stare, as if to say, 'Don't expect me to fetch that.'

Monty loves playing with other dogs and is a very sociable little character – in fact his only dislike is for Staffordshire terriers, following an incident when we were out in the park. A Staffordshire came after me, teeth bared, and I was terrified, absolutely shaking like a leaf. But Monty sensed my fear and my panic, and swiftly chased the dog away. Since then, any other Staffordshire terrier who comes near me gets the same treatment.

Monty has always been a favourite with the neighbours too. Everyone stops to talk to him when we are out and about, especially when he does his party trick of waving to them with his two front paws – it's adorable! He did his puppy foundation course when he was younger and passed with flying colours, which is probably why he gets on so well with humans and dogs alike.

Monty has a few funny habits. One is walking out of a room backwards if the floor is slippery or wet, and he really doesn't like it if my husband Martin and I are having a disagreement. He also enjoys getting under Mummy's duvet to keep warm. And he can be a very naughty West Highland terrier! He has a habit of finding our sweets and manages to open them up and eat them without eating the wrappers. I still don't know how he does this, even after all these years. He loves most food, like any dog, but biscuits are his favourite treat. He knows the word 'biscuits' very well!

Monty's character is mischievous, affectionate, loving, laid back, friendly, moody (sometimes), inquisitive, loyal, nosey, patient and protective. He sleeps a lot, especially on my bed, but likes his own space too, and especially loves going to the field at the back of our house. And he has a great love for his nana too.

Monty makes me feel so very happy, and loved. He is a great companion, and follows me everywhere, like my little shadow. Someone once told me that Monty is my guardian angel, and I truly believe that he is. He has given me so much support, making such an impact on my happiness and my health.

After an operation, I unfortunately picked up MRSA. I spent six months unable to see some of my closest family members – my nephew, who was about to have an operation himself, and my father, who was battling against lung cancer – and it was one of the loneliest times of my life. The only faces I saw daily were Martin's and Monty's, and concern for Monty's well-being was about the only thing that kept me going. It was such a difficult time, but I kept reminding myself that I had Monty to care for, so I pulled myself together and got on with life.

Monty means so much to me and has helped me overcome so many difficult periods of my life. He is always there for me, by my side no matter what has happened, never letting me down in thirteen years. He is my soul mate, my best friend, my guardian angel, and I love him to the moon and back with all my heart. I hope you enjoy reading about my special little dog and our life together as much as I have enjoyed writing about him.

Jennifer & Monty x

I work with all types of animals, but dogs share a special part of my heart. I like to show people just how amazing they are and how easy it is to connect on a deeper level, whether as part of training the dog's behaviour or just to develop a stronger bond. And the bond can be so strong with some people that the dogs may even come to be seen as surrogate children.

Now, before you feel this is a bad thing, let me tell you a story about a couple I came across about eight years ago. His name was David and she was called Annie. They had been childhood sweethearts and the bond between them was incredible. Having spent their early school years as friends, they fell madly in love. After a couple of years of marriage they were ready to start a family. Everyone around them expected this, and it was just something that was sure to happen.

However, it didn't quite work out that way. In fact, David and Annie couldn't conceive. They spent many years trying to have a baby and it still hadn't happened after medical intervention. This led Annie to suffer severe bouts of depression and David felt powerless to help her.

Then one day, when Annie was so low she had lost all interest in living, she looked out of her kitchen window to see a small cream figure sitting between the flower beds. Trying to focus, she could just make out two little eyes and a nose. As she looked at it, staring in fascination, the figure stared back. Annie went into the garden to investigate and found a small cream puppy staring up at her. He was only about six weeks old and looked totally lost. She just couldn't understand why such a pup would be in her flower bed!

Gathering him up into her arms, Annie took him into the house. He licked her nose in excitement and snuggled into her. Whether it was her motherly instincts or not, one thing was for sure: Annie's mood lifted. She wanted to nurture this little pup she had found. He needed her now, and actually she needed him too.

After the usual calls to local police and dog rescue centres there was still no clue about where he had come from that day and certainly no one wishing to claim him. So they named the little dog Alf and took him into their lives.

That need to nurture was paramount for Annie, and Alf lapped up the attention, loving his role within the family. He became a healing dog, helping Annie come to terms with how she was feeling. He made her laugh again, made her live again, but most of all made her love again. He was there at the moment she was thinking of taking her own life, and now he engulfed her life with the love she needed so badly.

David and Annie gave him all he required to meet his dog needs with an added twist of humanising. He soon became their surrogate child. Now, whilst I am not completely in favour of this, I saw with my own eyes how happy the three were. And Alf was certainly enjoying the role he was playing.

He needed the security, the love and connection they so freely gave.

The whole experience allowed Annie to look deeper within herself. She found herself in that little dog's heart. She and David had so much love to give, and they now foster and adopt pups and dogs in distress. It was good to see how life turned around for all three of them when little Alf appeared in the right place at the right time.

In my experience, dogs have a unique ability to turn people's lives around, no matter how bad they get, and this is why they are now used as part of therapy in hospitals, hospices and care homes.

For the last eight years or so I have been an official Pets As Therapy (PAT) assessor in Scotland for both dogs and cats. The charity sends dogs to people who are not able to see their own pets or who have lost animals when they were hospitalised or placed in a care home. A meeting with a therapy dog can make a tremendous difference to someone's life and happiness.

Each dog is chosen through a strict assessment, covering the temperament and personality, condition, and ability to communicate calmly with people, especially those that may be ill, and to co-operate with their handlers. Only the best dogs get through and go on to be therapy dogs. These dogs will visit the chosen venue perhaps a couple of times a month with their owner, cheering the lives of many at such desperate times. Just a pat and stroke of a therapy dog can lift the spirits of those who meet it.

The great thing about the dogs that do get through to becoming a PAT dog is that they absolutely love the job. They get into the routine of going to see the folk on a regular basis and totally love their visits, almost dragging their owners through the doors to meet their fan base! I am quite sure both the dogs and people involved get equal measures of happiness from the cuddles they receive.

Amazingly, there is a shortage of therapy dogs in the UK, with many hospitals, care homes and child and adult hospices awaiting a qualified dog to visit them. So please, if you think you have a dog that may suit and can spare a few hours a month to make someone's day, then contact Pets As Therapy and arrange an assessment for your dog.

Chapter Three

Over the years I have dealt with dogs of all shapes, sizes and personalities. There are dogs that adore humans and those that absolutely cannot stand them. They all have one thing in common, though: the willingness to talk! No matter how angry, scared or confused they are, they are more than happy to tell us communicators about it. When meeting dogs and reading them, you can sometimes help them and their people simply by highlighting this ability to communicate.

I once did a reading for a dog called Tom. He was happy in all areas of his life, and his owner just wanted to be sure that he was truly happy and not in need of anything. These types of readings are great to do, because you know the bond of trust and love between dog and owner is so strong and heartfelt.

Tom was a small to medium-sized whippet. He was fed well and walked well and over the years he had developed a strong, lean, athletic body. His coat was beautifully brindled in different shades of brown, tan and cream, with one strip of white starting from his nose and going up to, between and no further than his eye line.

As well as checking that Tom was happy, his owner also wanted to know if I really could talk with the dogs. I wouldn't say she was totally closed to the idea, but she was certainly very doubtful that it could be done. Her friends had suggested my services and she thought she would give it a go for Tom's sake. However, she wanted proof I was actually speaking with her dog and that I was not just some wacko making it all up.

Now, I have nothing to prove. I totally trust the information I get coming through. So for me this simple reading was to help Tom's owner understand that animals really do know what goes on around them and that they can communicate what they know. It was not necessarily for Tom's sake, as he was perfectly fine with life and his care.

Tuning into an animal always begins (well, ninety-nine per cent of the time) with my holding a photo of the pet in my hands. Tom was a sweet-looking dog with lovely eyes. I adore hounds. There is something about those long noses and kind eyes that melts me every time. Trust me when I say Tom was no exception. I melted instantly when looking at his photo. He was just beautiful, not only to look at, but in his soul, too. I felt it through every part of my body. He was a gorgeous dog and I would love to have the pleasure of being around him in person, but since I currently live in Scotland and he lives in New Zealand, the likelihood of us ever meeting in person is pretty slim. For now, though, I can use his photo to connect with him and have the pleasure of speaking with a beauty of a dog.

Tom's reading was pretty straightforward. He told me how happy he was, what he had for his meals and how well he was looked after by his owner. This is always good to hear, but for his owner I needed proof that I was really communicating with Tom and not just making this all up. So I asked him to give me three precise pieces of information that could validate the reading for her.

'Well, tell her about that stash of choccy she has hidden in the drawer in the bedroom,' he said. Then he added, 'And my name isn't Tom. She calls me Tom, but it's not my name. It's on the paper. She will tell you. She has it on the paper.'

I thanked Tom for the information and telephoned his mum with the results of the reading. His owner was really happy to hear that her dog was so content and happy. However, I could feel she was waiting for the proof I had promised her, and so I relayed the last bits of information Tom had given me about the choccy, as he called it, the name and the paper.

The phone line went quiet for a moment and for a second or two I thought I had lost her, until a quiet voice piped up, 'Oh my, Joanne. That's him. He can talk, he really can. I never believed it – well, not really. In fact I am in shock. Who else, I mean . . . How else would you know this? I'm fricken' freaked out right now! This is spooky stuff!'

'No, no, it's fine. Many people I speak to are just like you. Animal Communication is nothing to be scared of. It's to be celebrated. Your dog can communicate with humans, and how wonderful is that? So tell me, what does the information Tom gave me refer to?' I asked, smiling.

'Well, I keep choccy in the bottom drawer in my bedroom. That's chocolate to you and me, but I always say to Tom "Shh, don't tell anyone about the choccy!" It's my secret stash, you know, for when I need it. I say to him choccy, not chocolate. Oh my, how amazing! Hey, the sneak, he told you!' his owner shrieked in excitement.

'And you are absolutely right about his name,' she went on. 'His real name is Treasures of Thomas. Thomas was also his papa's name, and so we wanted to call him the same, in memory of his late papa, who was a very special dog in our family. Instead of Thomas we shortened it to Tom, but on his pedigree papers, which are here, Tom's full real name is Treasures of Thomas and his papa's name was Thomas the Great, so it's these papers he was telling you about. I often look at them and tell him what a special dog he is. Oh, Joanne, thank you so much,' she said, full of joy.

'You are more than welcome. And it wasn't me at all. It was all Tom, or should I say Thomas!' I laughed.

So there you go, even the most simple of readings can have a profound effect on an owner, giving them the brilliance of belief, and belief in something truly remarkable – Animal Communication.

I love meeting the owners when I do my workshops and watching their faces light up as they tell me all about their animals. Once they start they gush with love and admiration for their four-legged friends.

And dogs attend the workshops too, so that the students can work with them, which is great. The excitement when the dog walks into the room makes me giggle even to this day. No matter how down some people may be feeling or how tough life is, all their cares and worries wash away in an instant at that moment.

Not long ago I was hosting a workshop in the south of England. I had a group of about twenty people who were all eagerly awaiting the first case study of the day. At ten thirty there was a knock at the function suite door. In walked the most adorable pint-sized dog. His name was Archie and he was a cross between a Jack Russell and a wire-haired dachshund.

The cross had produced a really cute but odd-looking dog. He had a long body covered in a multitude of black and brown spots and patches, and his body was held up rather proudly by three (yes, I said three) short stumpy legs. The fourth, which was the left back one, had been neatly removed by a veterinary surgeon some time ago. This may seem tragic, but the little fellow was just as capable as any other dog as he marched in, wagging his tail and sniffing the air, delighted to meet his audience.

He may not have been the best-looking dog, but everyone in the room stopped and watched as he proudly tottered around to meet and greet everyone. One by one, looking each person in the eye, he said, 'Hello, I'm Archie.' Whilst most of the students couldn't hear his silent words, I and two others could hear him clearly.

'Pleased to meet you, Archie,' Jackie said, smiling down at him. Jackie is one of my students and an excellent communicator. She has been on two of my day courses so far, and studies with my home study course too. Her ability with horses and cats is rather fantastic, and one I am so very proud to be part of. The only issue with Jackie has been her own lack of self-belief. The problem seemed to lie mainly with her dog readings and it was holding her back so much. She was losing her self-esteem.

I saw Archie say hello to everyone. Then he turned around, walked across to where Jackie was sitting and sat neatly at her feet. His owner called him to sit with her, but the little dog just looked at her in defiance, and then looked up at Jackie. I could have sworn he winked at her!

It was now time for the group questions. We wanted to see how much information we could find out about Archie's life by using telepathic connection. Every student was to participate. One by one I suggested a question for them. I might say, 'Ask Archie what he had for breakfast,' and sure enough an image or word would pop straight into their mind and they would shout out in delight, 'Peanut butter on toast!' 'Correct!' gasped his owner in amazement.

I was paying particular attention to the way Archie was behaving with Jackie. Every time it was her turn to ask him a question, he would stare at her, not answer her question but instead ask her one, such as, 'Why are you this way?' or 'Why don't you let go? You know he's no good.' Jackie was quick to ignore the questions. She kept shaking her head and smiling, saying she wasn't getting a connection, but I could hear loud and clear, and secretly so could she.

I decided I needed to take matters into my own hands,

so I directed everyone but Jackie and little Archie to have a coffee break. 'Great work, guys. See you back here in fifteen minutes,' I smiled at my students.

Not wanting to pry too much, I asked Jackie's permission to listen in and help her with Archie and his questions. I could see her eyes welling up with tears as she nodded.

'I knew this was coming. I kept dreaming of a little dog just like Archie, and he kept pushing and pushing for the truth,' Jackie replied.

'Well, it's all meant to be, Jackie. Let's just see where it takes us. He obviously wishes to help you, so relax, no pressure,' I said, placing my hand on her left shoulder.

'Archie, what do you want to say to Jackie?' I asked him out loud.

'I know she is so sad and I want to help,' Archie replied, as quick as lightning.

'I heard that!' Jackie said, looking at me.

'Yes, me too. He's good, isn't he?' I smiled. In fact I had worked with Archie and his owner before. He is a very talkative dog and gets straight to the point when asked questions, which is good for students when they are learning the art of communication.

'So, Archie – how can you help Jackie?' I asked.

'She needs to let go. She is holding on to the past. Not good, not good. We all need to let go sometimes,' he said, as he scratched his ear with his only remaining back leg, almost toppling over as he did so.

'Let go of what, Archie?' I asked, whilst Jackie looked slightly uncomfortable at what was about to come.

'Her guilt,' he said. 'Her guilt for what happened.'

Jackie looked quite upset and I asked her if she was OK to carry on. She nodded, but I could see her face going a deeper shade of red and tears began steadily streaming down her cheeks.

'Are you sure you want to carry on?' I asked her.

'Yes,' she smiled, as Archie pushed his body into her legs as if to comfort her.

'It wasn't her fault. Make her understand,' he said, looking at me.

'What? What wasn't her fault?' I really didn't understand, but looking at the pair of them I knew they both knew exactly what was being talked about.

'He means the accident, Joanne,' she said, gulping. 'It was me. I did it. I knocked the dog over. The dog, it . . . it came from nowhere. I couldn't stop! It was four years ago and I still . . . I can't get it out of my head. He lives a street away. It's terrible. I avoid him all the time, but he keeps popping into my mind at all hours of the day. I try to ignore him, push him out. I just can't face it, Joanne, I just can't,' she sputtered.

Archie licked Jackie's hand and gave her a warm-hearted look.

'So you knocked down a dog? And it survived – that's good, isn't it?' I asked.

'He was like me,' Archie butted in. 'Just like me, and look how good I am! So it's OK, isn't it? She mustn't worry no more. Pointless!'

'I knocked this poor dog over and he lost one of his legs. It was all my fault,' she cried.

Archie was right. He was just like the dog Jackie had knocked down. He too had been involved in an accident and had lost his leg as a result, but he was just grateful to be alive. Nothing was going to stop him living life to the full.

'I just can't get it out of my head, Joanne. That's why I hold myself back from doing dog readings. I'm terrified the dog will come through and blame me for ruining his life.'

'Speak with him,' Archie said in a matter-of-fact voice.

'I agree with Archie, Jackie. It's time for you to face up to what has happened. Maybe if you speak with the dog you can get some closure?' I said.

'But what if his life is ruined because of me?' she asked.

'Doubt it . . . Look at mee!' Archie said.

We both looked down at Archie and giggled. He was lying on his back with all three legs sticking up in the air like an upside-down card table, private bits wiggling around in full view.

'Do you have to?' I laughed, pointing at the bits we really didn't wish to see.

He began wiggling his bottom as if to scratch his back on the carpet beneath him, then quickly sat up and gave a huge headshake sneeze.

'Just speak to the dog. He will be fine,' Archie said, and then wandered over to the chair on the opposite side of the room.

'Maybe I should, then?' Jackie replied, looking at me as if for my approval.

'Yes, Archie is absolutely right. For you to move forward in your communication you need to remove some issues, this being the main one. It's holding you back, Jackie, and, as he said, it needs to be dealt with.'

The door opened and in came the first three students, back from their coffee break, and Archie's owner.

'He hasn't been causing you any trouble, has he?' she laughed, pointing to Archie.

'Excuse me, dear!' Archie replied, sticking his nose in the air. Jackie and I both laughed.

'No, no. He's been a good boy and a great help,' I said, smiling.

Later that day, Jackie recalled the memory of the

accident in her mind, reliving every last detail as if slowly peeling the skin off an onion. As she gradually uncovered each layer of pain, hurt and trauma, the dog appeared to her. She could see him clearly in her mind. Instead of pushing the image out, as she usually did, she held on to it and began to allow herself to make a heartfelt connection.

Her first words were 'I'm so very sorry' and, as she told me through tears of sadness and joy over the phone, the dog replied, saying it was fine, he was OK, it was meant to be and that it was all his fault. He had run out across the road after being spooked by another dog, and she never stood a chance of missing him.

Jackie asked how the loss of the leg had affected his life, and his reply was totally unexpected.

'Well, I never really got much attention before the accident. I was just put out in the garden in the mornings. But now my people feel sorry for me so I'm allowed to sleep upstairs on the bed, and they feed me special meat in a tin. So it's totally fine. I'm happy. And I can still chase balls, too.'

Jackie felt so relieved that the dog seemed unaffected by the loss of his leg. He wasn't blaming her at all, as she had expected, and seemed to have no regrets. In fact, he was perfectly fine. She had done it. Jackie had finally made peace with her fear, the fear that had been holding back her work so much. Now she is able to do dog readings easily and is excelling in all areas of communication.

In my experience, animals will often surprise you. They do not always view situations in the way we expect, so communication is a great way of finding out the truth.

Dogs are remarkable in so many ways, and are often much stronger and more intelligent than we can ever imagine. And they have an incredible sense of awareness. A dog is an extraordinarily sentient being, capable of picking up distant energy and other frequencies far more easily than most humans and with far more depth and accuracy. It's something that scientists have tried to explain on many occasions, but the simple truth is they really can't get to the bottom of it. It's what I like to call 'sixth sense'.

Some of you may be laughing at this as you look at your own dog which may be, in your mind, one of the dimmest creatures that ever walked the earth (certain breeds of spaniel often come into this category). However, let me assure you that even the ones that seem to care about nothing but food can sometimes be more clever than they seem. I have clients who have been absolutely amazed at what their dogs have shown them or led them to discover through my communication work.

One instance involved an Old English sheepdog called Barney. Now, Barney was no ordinary dog. He was an active performer on stage and film and had appeared in many advertisements. Jane was in charge of Barney whenever he was on set and Jane's husband, Stan, would leave them to it, doing his own extra work on films elsewhere. This suited them both and it seemed Barney loved the work too. So all was happy.

Until I got a phone call from Jane one day. She was beginning to worry about Barney's behaviour when on set. He was a great dog normally, but now he seemed to be getting stressed and barking at various cast members.

They were in their first two weeks of filming a television drama which they would be working on for between six and twelve weeks. Her husband had a part in the same drama and this was the first time they had worked on set together. Jane wondered whether it could be something to do with her husband being there too, because Barney was fine when he was alone with her. She had called me in to see if I could find out what the problem was. She also mentioned that she and her husband hadn't been getting on too well of recent months and now, with Barney's behaviour affecting his work, the strain was beginning to show.

'Tell me what he tells you, Joanne. Everything. I want the truth. If it's my fault I need to know. Promise me you will tell me the truth,' Jane begged me.

'Of course I will, but I'm sure you have done nothing wrong. Perhaps he is just stressed. Maybe he's had enough of being in the limelight. Some dogs do. They are fine for years, then one day they wake up and can't deal with the work any more. Just like some human actors, it can happen to animals too,' I replied.

So I did the reading, and when I tuned into Barney using my communication ability this is what happened.

'Hi, Barney. My name is Joanne and I would like to talk with you. Would that be OK?' I asked, hoping the answer would be yes.

'Suppose so,' came the reply.

'Your mum, Jane, says you are uncomfortable on set at the moment. Are you OK? Is something making you unhappy?' I asked him.

'Yes,' he said quickly.

'Yes? What do you mean? Can you explain to me in a little more detail?'

'It's him,' he replied.

'Who?' I asked. But as soon as I said the word 'who' I felt an instant connection with Jane and saw a picture in my mind's eye of her husband (I had previously seen photos of him). 'Your human dad?' I asked. 'Is this the person you are not happy with?'

'Yes. And her,' he said.

'Her being your human mum, Jane?' I replied, trying to get to why he would be unhappy with both of them. After all, Jane had said he was fine around her.

'No,' he snapped.

'No? So not your human mum, Jane?' I questioned.

'Her, the one that has the long coat,' he said.

'Long coat?' I asked, slightly confused.

'Yes, like my human mum,' he replied.

I thought for a moment. I had known Jane for some time and, as far as I was aware, I had never seen her wearing a long coat. She always wore stylish cropped jackets, showing off her amazing waist. They were sometimes leather, sometimes denim, but never long. Then it struck me – did he mean her hair, which was really long like mine?

'Barney, do you mean a long coat like mine?' I asked him, pointing to my hair.

'Yes, just like yours,' he replied.

'So why are you unhappy with her – or him, for that matter? Where's the problem, Barney?' I still had no idea who the lady might be, or why he had a problem with either of them.

'Three o'clock,' came his reply.

'What about three o'clock?' I asked.

'That's when they go,' he said.

'Go where?' I asked, still feeling puzzled.

'Home. I smell them,' came his reply.

'I don't understand, Barney. Can you help me understand a little more, please?' I asked him, knowing that if you ask the animals to explain in more detail they often will.

'Three o'clock, they leave to go home. My home, my human mum's home. We stay, we work. They go,' he said.

'Together?' Feeling a knot start to develop in my tummy, I suddenly thought I knew where this was heading and I didn't like it. 'So this is what is making you unhappy? Can I look into it, Barney? Let me try and help,' I replied.

'Tell my mum,' he replied and then the connection we had was lost.

I thought about it for a while and decided to call Jane and tell her what Barney had said in his reading. I needed to tell her the truth. She had asked me to do so and I had promised to tell her everything.

'Jane, I have spoken with Barney,' I began, and then told her exactly what he had told me in the reading.

'I knew it! I bloody well knew it!' she snapped.

'Knew what?' I asked.

'Valerie! Bloody Valerie London. She had a fling with my husband about nine years ago. I forgave him then as he told me she had seduced him and it was a one-off. Then when he got this job, he said he was unaware she would be here too! He told me it was all over and that it was purely professional. I knew it!' she said angrily.

'Oh, Jane, I'm not suggesting your husband is having an affair. I'm just relaying what Barney has told me,' I said.

'Well, Barney said three o'clock, didn't he?' she asked.

'Umm, yes,' I replied.

'Well, that's about right, Joanne. Because for the last week they have both finished shooting their scenes at two thirty and then we have to stay until late in the evening to do ours, along with other cast members. So the two of them would in fact be away together at about three o'clock!'

'Listen, it may be something completely different to what you are thinking, so please, just be careful,' I suggested. But I knew Jane. Once she got the bit between her teeth, so to speak, she wouldn't let go.

'Joanne, thank you. Or I suppose I should be saying thank you to Barney, eh?' She laughed more calmly.

Three days went past and I hadn't heard from Jane. I was about to call to make sure she was OK when I received a text from her on my mobile.

'Joanne, are you OK to talk?' Jane asked.

I sent a text back saying of course I was, and the phone immediately began to ring.

'Joanne, it's me, Jane.'

'Hi, Jane. Is everything OK? I was actually about to . . .' And before I could say 'I was about to phone you' she told me what had happened.

'I want to say a huge thank you to you – well, Barney, really. Joanne, he was right!'

Jane explained that, on the next day of filming, she had taken along a friend who was also a dog handler. Without telling her husband, she left at three o'clock, just behind him, leaving Barney with her friend to carry on his filming duties.

She was secretly following her husband's car back towards her home when she caught sight of the woman she had mentioned to me, Valerie London, also driving towards her home. Parking in a quiet part of her street and hiding low behind the steering wheel like someone in a detective series, she watched as both Valerie and her husband got out of their cars and entered the house – Jane's house!

She decided not to confront them that day, as she was too emotional. She was in so much shock and anger that she feared she would do something bad to one or even both of them. So instead Jane drove back to the studio, phoned her husband and made up a story about staying over with Barney at her friend's home for the night. She said she would meet him at work the next day.

The next day arrived. Once again her friend the dog handler was with her and, just as she had done the day before, Jane secretly sneaked out after her husband had left for the day. She watched her husband and Valerie go into her home, but this time she waited for an hour before quietly letting herself in through the back door.

She walked quietly around the house and, not finding them downstairs, proceeded upstairs to her bedroom. With one sweep of her arm she opened her bedroom door to find Miss London in a not so ladylike position, along with her husband, who had a look of horror on his face.

'Oh, that's terrible!' I said. 'What did you do?'

'Well, I stood there as calmly as possible, said nothing, and just stared at the two of them,' she laughed.

'You sound so calm, Jane. Are you sure you are OK?' I asked. I was slightly concerned at the cool manner in which Jane was telling me all this.

'Hey, I think it was worse for them. They looked horrified at me finding them like that! For me, I have known something was up for a long time, but had no proof. So I finally got it, and to see them both squirm at the embarrassment of the situation was more than enough for me, Joanne, let me tell you,' Jane replied. 'Also, Miss London has stretch marks like the map of Britain! Made me feel great! So she's not Miss Perfect after all. They are welcome to each other,' Jane laughed.

Needless to say, that was the end of that marriage. Jane's dog, Barney, went back to being his normal lovable self and they were happy again. But be careful what you get up to when there are dogs around. Barney certainly knew what Jane's husband was doing behind her back. It just goes to show, these dogs are capable of knowing far more than most people give them credit for!

Thankfully for me, this sort of thing doesn't happen too often in my readings but it certainly reminds you of the strength of the human and animal bond. Barney was definitely looking out for his mum, Jane.

It's not just people who possess telepathic skills, although we often hear about these. No, it's dogs too. Your dogs, my dogs, in fact every dog on the planet. They all have the ability to send and receive messages to and from each other and through to human beings too.

Now, the question is, Do we actually listen?

Receiving a dog's message can be as simple as 'just knowing', or you may suddenly have a picture of something in your mind's eye. Perhaps you see your dog's water bowl being empty, for example. When you go and look, sure enough the bowl is empty, and you ask yourself, How did I know this? What made me think it was empty? How and why did I get that image in my mind of the empty water bowl?' Well, the answer is quite simple: your dog was thirsty and he sent you a really clear message that he needed water. And that is what we call a telepathic exchange. Because you have a connection with love, which I call 'the love link', you and your dog can send and receive telepathic messages.

I work using telepathic connections, so I am well tuned in to the dogs' messages. I may hear them whilst doing a simple reading for someone's pet, or receive messages from my own dogs. I teach my students how to identify when their dog is trying to tell them something, and this is something you can learn too. Often, a dog who seems to be behaving badly is actually in distress and asking for help.

I came across a dog called Max at a recent workshop. He was a liver and white cocker spaniel and his owner assured me that he was in fact absolutely stupid. Independent, self-centred, non-emotional and a true little horror, he was constantly getting up to no good. He barked at nothing, drove the neighbours crazy, chewed everything in sight and generally made it his job to be naughty for no apparent reason whenever he was with her.

I wanted to find out more about this dog. Surely he couldn't be as bad as his owner made out? So I asked to have some quiet time alone with him, just me and the dog. I did this during the lunch hour, with no distractions and no outside influence.

'Max, will you talk with me?' I asked. But the dog was unsettled, wouldn't calm down and just kept pacing around the floor.

'Max, please,' I said gently, and I sent calming thoughts through my mind to help relax him. For a brief moment I wondered if indeed the owner was right. Perhaps he had some sort of brain disorder. He certainly looked as if he was on another planet, and not one I was on.

Suddenly he walked straight up to me and looked me right in the eye. 'She can't go,' he said quickly. It was so quick that I only just caught the words.

'Go? Go where?' I asked.

He began pacing around again and pawing at the carpet. Even I felt agitated being around him.

Back came the answer: 'Work.'

'What do you mean, she can't go to work?' I asked.

'She can't leave me again. I can't deal with it. I worry too much. It makes me sick,' he said, spinning around and letting out a shriek of a bark at the door.

I looked at the dog in front of me and felt a wash of emotion come over me. Sure enough, his heart was absolutely bouncing. My body felt like I had pins and needles all over my skin and I was feeling panicky.

'Max, calm down. Can you explain what is happening?' I asked.

'She goes back, I will die. They said,' he snapped.

'What? Who said?' I asked, shocked at what he had said.

'The man. He said, if she goes, it is kinder for me to go,' he said, shaking uncontrollably.

I thought for a moment, trying to comprehend his words. Why on earth would his mum have the dog put to sleep just because she was going to work? It didn't make sense.

I called his owner back into the room, and told her what he had told me. She shook her head in disbelief. 'No, no, no. I cannot believe he is thinking this. He's got it all wrong.'

'So what is he going on about?' I asked, hoping she knew, because for once I was stumped.

'He suffers from what the vet calls separation anxiety. When I leave him to go to my work he completely goes to pieces, and I mean completely. He screams the house down, chews, shakes. In fact, he falls apart, really. I work for a major clothing brand and often have to make trips to the States for a week at a time. I leave Max with my sister, but he struggles to cope. Won't eat, drink or function like a normal dog. I went to the vet to see if there was anything else we could try and he said, because of the severity of the condition, if he showed no signs of improvement after working with behaviourists, we might have to consider putting him out of his misery, because I am going to be away more and more this year with work.' She began crying as she told me all this.

'Well, look, he is so bad that I am not sure I can help. But we have to try. We have no other choice,' I replied.

First, I needed to look at why Max was getting so worried. It couldn't just be because his owner was leaving him. There had to be more to it. I wanted to see them both at home, and we made an appointment for later that week so that I could meet them again in their own surroundings.

Arriving at the address, I found what I can only describe as a very cold, lonely flat. All the walls were painted a pale white, the chairs were white leather, there were no cushions on the sofa and no rugs on the bare white wooden floors. It was so sterile that I was absolutely amazed Max's owner would even have a dog in the flat.

I watched as Max followed her every move, shaking and whining whenever she got up to move. She was absolutely right. He just couldn't cope when she made any attempt at all to leave him.

I decided to use some intuition and communication. First I asked his owner how often she was away, and for how long. Then I relayed this information back to Max and asked him if he understood time. 'Sort of. It goes so long,' he replied.

When an animal does not understand time, I use the term 'sleep', either saying it verbally or visualizing the night-time scenario, so each night the owner is expected to be away from home, a 'sleep' equals one night. For instance, if you were away two nights you would say to your animal, 'I am going to be away from you for two sleeps. That way your animal will understand when you are expected back. So I sent Max an image of a 'sleep', and he got it straightaway. OK, I was now getting through. I asked his owner if she had ever told him that she was going and when she was coming back.

She looked at me blankly and said, 'Joanne, he's a dog! I only came along to the workshop because I was worried his behaviour was getting worse, and I heard you could correct it.'

'Well, perhaps. But first you need to play along with me and do as I ask, no matter how stupid it sounds to you. Just trust me, please, will you?' I smiled, hoping she would accept.

'This stuff is weird, but hey, what have I got to lose?'

'Max, that's what. I don't think he can cope much more,' I said, pointing to the dog lying down near her, still shaking uncontrollably. 'Where does he sleep?' I asked.

'On the floor. He likes it, always has,' she said, slightly confused.

'Has he ever had a bed? Or maybe he could sleep on the sofa?' I said.

'Oh, god, no – not on my sofa. And I never got a bed for him because I couldn't find one in plain white and he seemed quite happy on the floor,' she explained.

I told her that all dogs need somewhere of their own to retreat to, somewhere where they will feel comforted and safe, and advised that a dog bed with a soft cushion was essential. She didn't look happy, but she did purchase a new soft and cosy dog bed, even though it went against what she wanted to do.

I then worked with her to tell Max when she was going and for how long, using the technique of one day equals one sleep, so Max would be fully aware when she was coming back. As she was due to be away for twelve days, we sent Max the communication that his owner would be away from him for twelve sleeps.

He began to cope again. He knew she was coming back to him and so was able to get into his bed and count the number of sleeps until her return. We combined the communication with some essential oil therapy, something that was designed for stress and anxiety.

The combination worked. He no longer felt alone and scared. He settled down and became a relaxed dog. His behaviour changed so much that even the vet was amazed. And all it came down to was a simple need to know what was happening. Every time she went away for work, he was thinking she was leaving him for good. No one had told him when or if she would ever return, and so panic set in. Within months Max was fine.

Just the other day I had a lady phone me up, half laughing, half frustrated. 'Joanne, will you please tell her to stand still,' were her first words. Not 'Hello', or 'Hi, I need help'. I could hear her frustration and wondered what on earth was going on.

'Umm, yes, so what's the problem?' I asked.

'I am trying to groom Maddie and she just won't stand still. I have to be at work at three o'clock and it's two thirty now. Please, Joanne, can you just do this for me?' she asked, sounding desperate.

'Yes, of course I will try. Is this Maddie the cairn terrier?'

I asked, thinking it might be a dog I had connected with about a month previously.

'Yes, the Pets As Therapy dog,' the lady answered.

'Ah, yes, I know. Is she going somewhere?' I asked.

'Yes, we need to be at the hospital for three o'clock to do our work. She needs a brush and she just won't let me,' she cried.

I asked her to calm down and relax, because if you are tense, your dog will be too. On the other hand, if you take some deep breaths your dog will pick up on your energy and calm.

Then I asked Maddie if she would let her owner give her a quick brush as she had a very important job to do, and her reply was this: 'Tell her I am not having that comb on my back. My hair will fall out.'

'Maddie says she does not want that comb on her back as it will make her hair fall out,' I told her owner.

'Her hair? Why would she say that?' her owner asked.

So I asked Maddie and she told me that she had overheard a young lady in the hospital the week before saying that when she combed her hair it all fell out. I relayed this information to her owner, who confirmed they had visited a cancer ward the week before. One of the patients had been talking about her treatment and recalling the moment when her hair came out in clumps as she combed it.

'No, Maddie, your hair will not come out. You are going to be fine. The young lady had treatment that made that happen, but you will be OK. It's good to comb your hair. You need to look your best. So will you now stand for your owner to comb you? I promise nothing will happen but nice things,' I told her.

'Joanne, she is standing! Thank you so much. What a silly dog she is!' the lady replied. 'Got to dash. Thanks again, Joanne. Love from us both.' And with that she was gone.

It always amazes me how animals can overhear a conversation and worry that what they have heard will happen to them. Association can play a big part in their well-being. They can fear things too, just like humans, so it's great to be able to put them at rest about their worries.

When using communication, you may not always understand the consequences of what you are asking your dog to do – they may not turn out to be what you expected! I found this out for myself with my own dog Rosie, my beautiful red and white borzoi bitch.

Rosie is a bright cookie, smart, intelligent and a real mummy's dog. We have a unique connection. She loves to please me and is the most loyal dog that I could ever ask for. So when my young borzoi male dogs were here, Rosie would see herself as superior. And in my eyes, whilst I loved them all the same, she certainly was my special girl. I obviously adore her.

Rosie was a show dog from the beginning and was very successful. With her stunning conformation and movement, she proudly became one of the top borzois in the UK, gaining the title of champion very quickly. Rosie has five challenge certificates and five reserve challenge certificates, numerous championship best hound wins and many other first prizes.

So she was a great bitch to produce the next generation of superb puppies, in temperament, conformation and type. I am not a breeder and certainly wouldn't have a litter of puppies for the sake of it, but Rosie was such a special borzoi that the right thing to do was to carry the genetic lines on and continue to produce the best in the breed. All the puppies would have homes to go to as I had a waiting list of exhibitors of the breed wanting Rosie's puppies.

Now, this all sounds simple, doesn't it? When Rosie was old enough we would find a suitable dog and puppies would be born into this world. However, I made a huge mistake with my communication that embedded deep in Rosie's brain.

Rosie and my male dogs, Mozart, Mosko and Ruben, all lived alongside each other and so Rosie, being the only bitch, needed to keep her wits about her when it came to her seasons. (As you are probably aware, this is the time when a dog and bitch can mate, which usually lasts for around three weeks in total, twice per year.) The best time is normally on or around the thirteenth day of the season.

So all the time Rosie was young, knowing she was too young and not ready to have puppies, I'd say, 'Rosie, don't let the boys near your ladybum!' and laugh, knowing she would understand what I meant. I said this anytime the boys went anywhere near her.

Of course when she was first in season I'd separate them, but there were times she had to be near them, for instance when we were in the car or cleaning the kennels out, so I made it quite clear they were not to go near her. Being the smarty-pants she is, Rosie took note of this and whenever the boys came anywhere near her she'd give them a quick look of disapproval. If they didn't back off, she simply raced over to me and looked at me with disgust that they wouldn't listen. This went on for a few years and I knew I never had to worry about them. She was fiercely strict and stuck to what I had asked her to do.

This was great until the day came when she had won so much at the championship shows that the time was right to mate her with a handsome young dog called Hugo. I selected him carefully and he was a perfect match for her: a tall cream and white dog, with perfect conformation and temperament and great breeding lines that matched Rosie's. They were sure to produce some of the most fabulous puppies the borzoi exhibitors had seen.

But my plan backfired. Rosie had learnt to keep my males away, but now she extended this to all males, including unfortunately the handsome, devastatingly charming Hugo!

What I had originally thought would keep her safe from becoming pregnant in her early years had now become so stuck within her mindset that no male would ever be able to get near her. And so puppies were simply out of the question: she was having none of it. No amount of communication on my part could get her to change her mind. She was not having any of the plan, and that was that. My one and only amazing bitch was never to have puppies.

Over the years many people have asked why on earth I never bred from Rosie (who is now too old for breeding) and I just had to say, 'She doesn't want to have sex. Communication can be a powerful contraception tool, so be careful how you use it!' They gave me puzzled looks, thinking I was totally crazy, but my words were the truth.

I suppose there are breeders who would have forced their dogs to perform, but this has never and would never be an option for me with any of my dogs, especially Rosie. I love her, so why would I even contemplate such a thing? You wouldn't do it to a human, so why a dog? Animals have emotions and suffer heartache just as we do and can be traumatised just as we can, so it is my belief that forcing them to breed is never the right thing to do.

I recently received an email from a gentleman who was very proud to say he had a clever dog on his hands. His dog did a party trick. But as I read on I realised all was not what it seemed. This is what he wrote:

Dear Joanne,

I noticed the other day you were talking about dogs with special talents on the local radio station, and thought I would send this email over to you. My dog, Bounty, has a real special talent that makes me and my friends laugh all the time. He is a five-year-old dark brindle boxer, full of fun, and he loves to be the centre of attention.

Bounty will wait until everyone is in the room, wander in and then, just like the dog Brian on the comedy show *Family Guy*, he walks along the floor on his bottom from one side of the room to the other whilst holding the gaze of myself or my friends. He does it over and over in front of them whenever they come to visit. It's hilarious!

Just thought you'd like to hear this. He's a great dog.

Thanks,

Mark

Aghh! He isn't doing a party trick! He is trying to get someone's attention because he is actually suffering from worms or a build-up of his anal glands. This dog is raising the alarm bells. His action is a call for help, not a trick.

Obviously I sent an email straight back and explained that he needed a visit to the vet, ASAP. Thankfully Mark took notice and Bounty was soon sorted out by a vet. It was indeed his anal glands causing him trouble but he only needed a simple procedure and all was well.

Please take notice when your animals behave in an abnormal way. OK, there are some exceptions who are just crazy dogs, but normally if dogs show us an unusual behaviour there is an issue. So always be aware and get them checked out by a vet. If nothing is wrong and their health is fine, then you can call it a party trick!

I particularly remember one occasion when I was able to use my ability to hear the messages animals send. It took place with a wonderful rescue-centre dog, a big, beautiful, honey-coloured cross-breed with dark, deep chestnut eyes that would melt your heart.

It was one of those days when I had little to do. (Believe me, they don't happen very often!) My fiancé's sister Ruth came round to my house to see if I fancied practising some communication skills. She had recently been to one of my workshops and was keen to try out some new techniques with me.

Not wanting to stay in the house, I suggested we try outdoor communication, and we decided to go along to our local dog shelter, where we could chat to some willing subjects. I often advise my students to practise with rescue animals, most of whom see communicators as a welcome relief and are only too pleased that someone is listening to them.

When we arrived at the shelter the ladies at reception granted us access to the kennels, where we were greeted with a barrage of barking, howling and wolf-like yowls.

'How on earth can you hear anything with all this noise?' Ruth asked, with her fingers plugged into her ears.

'Well, if they wish to speak with you, they will,' I replied.

We walked round each kennel and sent out oodles of love

and hope to the dog in each kennel, using our love-link connection. There were dogs of all shapes and sizes, with long hair, short hair and even one with no hair! Some looked sad, some were happy and a few were just outrageous. We spent time with all of them. Each dog has its own story to tell.

However, there was one particular dog that I noticed from a distance. Whenever someone walked up to her she would take off like a ball of fire and throw herself at the bars of the cage. I was at least forty feet away but already I could hear her. It was as if all the background noise parted in my brain and in came a voice saying, 'Speak to me.' They were the clearest words I had heard for quite some time. The strange thing was, even though she looked like a caged monster, the voice was soft, clear and emotional. I stood for a couple of minutes, to make sure my hearing was correct, and to let two couples walk (or, rather, run) past her. I think she scared them half to death.

Ruth was busy being chatted up by a handsome terrier, who was using his charm to keep her at his kennel. And it was working, because she was oblivious to me heading in the direction of the mad dog who was sending people fleeing in fear! As I approached her kennel she was almost foaming at the mouth whilst giving her last warning to the people going past.

'Hey, you,' I whispered gently.

She suddenly turned round, took one look at me and leapt into the air. I jumped away and nearly fell over backwards! Suddenly there was silence. She had jumped towards me, but only to push her body close up to the cage so she could talk to me.

'Hello,' she said. She didn't bark, growl or throw herself against the bars. She just sat quietly and spoke to me.

'Hi, you are very beautiful,' I replied. I always like to start a conversation with something positive like a compliment. 'Why were you barking at those people so aggressively?' I asked her.

'Because I wanted you to come,' she replied.

'What is your name?' I asked.

'Jenny,' she replied, 'but they keep calling me Gypsy. That isn't my name.'

'Jenny it is, then,' I smiled.

'I'm misunderstood,' she announced.

'Why?' I asked.

'They have misunderstood,' she kept saying over and over.

I kept wondering why she was feeling misunderstood, so I decided to ask her and hoped for an answer.

'They think I have bitten my friend, but I never did,' she answered.

'OK, so why are you here, then?' I asked.

'They say I have bitten him, but I didn't. I don't know why I am here. I'm misunderstood.'

I knew this dog didn't have a clue why she was in the rescue centre, so I decided to read her card, which was on the far end of the kennel. To my amazement it read:

Gypsy must not be homed with other dogs, has bitten before, no children or cats. Some behaviour training needed. Experienced home only.

This certainly wasn't the dog I was chatting to. She was sweet, kind and intelligent. I decided I would find out a little more about her personality to see if any of the description added up.

'Do you like to play with toys, Jenny?' I smiled.

'Yes, yes I do, especially my yellow ball,' she said with excitement.

At that point I was clearly hearing her words (clairaudience), and I was also seeing a picture of a tennis ball in my mind (clairvoyance). She had described it as yellow, and I thought tennis balls were white, but I could clearly see a yellow tennis ball. And I was experiencing her feelings of joy about her favourite toy (clairsentience). (I will tell you more about these terms in the last chapter of this book.)

By this time Ruth had finally managed to tear herself

away from the little gigolo and was heading my way. I waved to her to stay where she was, and explained to Jenny that I would be back to talk to her in a minute or two.

As I walked up to Ruth, I asked her to observe the dog I had just been talking to. And, sure enough, as soon as another unsuspecting couple appeared at her kennel she exploded, scaring off yet another potential new family.

'Woah, she's mental!' Ruth said.

I disagreed and explained what I had heard, inviting Ruth to come and meet Jenny for herself.

Ruth walked up to the kennel, anticipating that Jenny would go ballistic, as she had just witnessed, but to her complete surprise she came and sat quietly next to us, with her nose pushed through the bars. Ruth was as amazed as I had been when she read Jenny's kennel card. It just did not correspond to the beautiful canine that was sitting with us.

One of the kennelmaids noticed us giving this particular dog a lot of our attention and headed over, probably thinking we were prospective owners for this so-called aggressive animal. This was the perfect opportunity to find out why Jenny was in the shelter.

To our surprise, it turned out that Jenny's owner had brought her into the shelter stating that her two dogs didn't get on and that she had to keep them in separate rooms or else they would kill each other. She had said her name was Gypsy and so the staff had carried on calling her this, but weirdly the dog did not respond. The kennelmaid also said that they had tried Gypsy with other dogs and had seen no sign of aggression at all.

'What's her favourite toy? If she has one,' I asked.

'Oh, yes, she does. There it is, behind her bed. She loves it!' she laughed.

Ruth and I stared, for there behind her bed was a tennis ball! And it was bright yellow!

That was all the validation we needed. I explained the situation to the kennelmaid and hoped and prayed she would take on board all the information this dog had given us.

I also explained to Jenny that she had indeed been misunderstood, that her name would be changed to Jenny on her kennel card and she would have the chance of a new loving home.

She understood.

A few weeks later I returned to check on Jenny and, to my delight, she had been very happily rehomed – and with another dog! So it was a happy ending for a lovely dog.

Chapter Four

How many times have you experienced knowing the phone is about to ring and, better than that, knowing who is going to be on the other end – and you are right? Or perhaps you think something in your own mind and then out of the blue a family member or partner comes out with the exact same thought? Well, that's telepathic connection.

I believe that this is easy enough at close range, for instance with family and people that you know well, but it can also happen with complete strangers when they are in need, be they human or animal. One of the most profound experiences of my entire career as a professional Animal Communicator was an instance of a distant telepathic cry for help, and it occurred just recently. Reliving this through writing about it is a little difficult for me. However, I think it's important I share the story with you.

Out of the blue, I began feeling a plea for help. It had been going on for around four days, and I couldn't quite understand where it was coming from. The feeling of utter desperation kept coming over me in waves of emotion that I was unable to ignore and it certainly wasn't coming from any of the animals I was currently working with. But the fact I didn't know or couldn't find out who it was tested my psychic ability to the limit. I was stumped, no matter how much I tried. No answers came back when I asked telepathically who was calling to me. I tried to visualise and develop a picture in my mind, but nothing came. I couldn't see or hear anything, but this heartfelt plea was aching through my veins.

Time will tell, I told myself, trying to come to terms with the fact that I was currently powerless to help what or whoever it was that was in trouble. In fact, I wasn't even sure if it was human or animal.

A few days passed and I received a phone call from my seventy-two-year-old mum, who lives on her own apart from her very noisy bird, Charlie. Recent events with some rowdy youths had spooked her a little and so Mum was phoning to ask if I thought she should get a dog. She was not really looking for protection, but more for companionship. And perhaps she would feel a bit safer just knowing that the dog would bark and she would be pre-warned if anyone were to break into her home.

I thought this was a perfect idea as my mum missed having a dog in the house, and I also thought perhaps it would give her something to focus her life on, make her take some exercise to keep her fit and provide a companion she could share times with.

Mum asked me what breed she should get and began suggesting Labradors, retrievers and other larger breeds. Whilst they are all lovely, I thought the size would be too much for her to handle. My mum is certainly fit – she still walks to town around a mile from her home and dances around the living room to Elvis Presley songs like she is twenty-one again! – but I just felt a larger dog was too much. I suggested she find a small one that would be a little lighter on the lead, but she was having none of it. To my mum, a dog has to be large, not a little lapdog, which just doesn't do anything for her. Then, in an instant, the word 'lurcher' came to my mind. I'm not sure why or where it came from, but it did. My mum paused and replied excitedly, 'Yes, a lurcher. Perfect!'

My mother had grown up with whippets, greyhounds and lurchers from an early age. Her grandparents raced them, and as a little girl my mum was often roped in to help train the lurchers at the local park. She would hold them by their collars whilst her granddad ran ahead with a lure made from an old rag with fur from a rabbit tied to it. When he was far enough away he would signal for her to let go of the dog and off it ran at full speed to catch the lure. So the breed was one that she was familiar with and had fond memories of as a child. It was a perfect choice for her: not too big, not too small, light on the lead and very loyal and loving, making a great companion.

It was decided that a puppy would be out of the question, due to my mum's age, and so we agreed I would look for an older dog that needed a quiet home. Trusting my ability to find the right dog for her, my mum left me to it and so the next day I went onto the Internet to look for rescue lurchers that needed a new home. It was strange, every time I typed in 'rescue lurchers', using various descriptions, something else would catch my eye. It was a breeder's website, not a rescue centre. Not wishing to purchase a puppy, I tried to ignore it.

After a while I still hadn't found the right dog through any of the rescue sites and I finally decided to have a nosey at the breeder's site, just out of curiosity. I wasn't expecting to find a dog, but I adore the breed too, and I suppose I was thinking it would be fun to look at the photos of the dogs, to admire their colours and remind myself how beautiful this crossed breed is.

As I clicked onto the first page I thought to myself, This is a nice, well laid-out website. Everything was in order, and it looked very professional and inviting. Then I clicked on the gallery pictures to see the dogs they currently had in their care. As I scrolled down through the images I could see each dog in the perfect working stance. They looked in clean condition but something about their faces made me feel sad.

That wave of desperation washed over me again just as it had been doing for the last few days. Each dog looked perfect, but sad. Now, those of you who know lurchers as a breed will know that they have very soulful eyes and you will often hear people comment on how sad they look, but this feeling was different. I couldn't explain it.

I decided to come off the site and take another look around the following day to see if there were any new rescue lurchers on the sites for rehoming. No new dogs appeared the next day, and the ones that were available were either too wild for my mum to handle or they were too young. Ideally, I was looking for a calm older dog or bitch that just needed a quiet forever home. Then, up popped the breeder's website link again, just as it had the day before. I thought for a moment and, as I felt more and more drawn to it, I decided to give the breeder a ring. She might know of an old retired dog that was looking for a home.

I telephoned the number in front of me and began to feel

uneasy. Why? Well, at the time I wasn't sure. I knew I was drawn to the website, and I also knew that it kept popping up more often than any of the others. I felt a pull, a kind of need to contact, but that was it. You could say my heart was pulling me in, like a deep longing for a loved one.

'Hello, is that Hilary of Graceland Lurchers?' I asked politely.

'Yes. Why?' the caller on the other end snapped, taking me aback a little. She didn't seem friendly at all.

'My name is Joanne, and I wonder if you could help me?' I asked, hoping she wouldn't snap again.

'What? What is it?' she continued to snap. 'What do you want?'

'I am looking for a lurcher for my mum, an older one if possible. Perhaps a retired breeding bitch, one that just needs a good home. Do you have any or know anyone who has?' I asked, hoping for a positive reply.

The phone went silent for a few minutes, and then I heard her yell at something to get off before she answered.

'Umm, I may have what you want. I've an old quiet bitch here. She's ten, used to be my best breeding bitch. She's a little skinny at the moment, but you can take her if you want.'

I was obviously really pleased, firstly because she was older and secondly she was quiet. The weight certainly wouldn't be a problem – my mum would soon get her looking in tip-top condition.

'How much do you want for her?' I asked, hoping it wouldn't be too much. After all, she was ten years old and no spring chicken.

'Two hundred pounds,' the breeder replied quickly.

'Umm, two hundred is a little more than I had expected to pay. Would you accept a hundred? She will be going to a lovely forever home, I can promise you that,' I said, trying to reassure the breeder and hoping this might make a difference.

'Fine. One hundred. When will you come and get her? I am busy, you know!' she snapped again.

And without even thinking of logistics, I quickly replied, through fear of losing the deal, 'Oh, I can be with you tomorrow afternoon if that's OK with you?'

'I will text over the address as it's not on the website. Be here for four o'clock.' And with that the lady hung up the phone.

Now, I would never advise anyone to purchase a dog in a hurry. You must always take your time. Make sure you view the parents, if possible, and seek out all the information you can find about its background. Try and spend a little time with it to make sure you match personalities. My advice is: do not rush into buying any dog, no matter how cute. But this time I went against my own advice. I did something I would never normally do and said straightaway I'd take the dog. I just had a feeling inside she was meant to be.

The worst of it was that I hadn't once thought to find out where in the country the breeder was situated. It wasn't until she sent me the full address via text that I realised. The address was miles away. I live in Scotland and she was not far from the Midlands area. But I did think it would be OK, as it was only about forty minutes from where my mum lived, which was a stroke of luck.

The plan was to drive down first thing in the morning, collect the lurcher and then take her directly to my mum's house. That way she could settle straight in. So actually, whilst it was nearly a six-hour journey for me, it would be worth it. My mum would be over the moon with happiness and the old dog would have a lovely new life.

The next morning I phoned my friend Yvonne and she agreed to come with me to the breeder's. That way she could hold the dog, if need be, whilst we were travelling from the breeder's to my mum's house. On the way down we stopped off at the local pet shop, and purchased a new soft dog bed that would fit a lurcher with no problems, two new bowls for water and feed, a big bag of the best dog food on the market, shampoo, a new pink lead and collar, worming tablets as I suspected this could be the cause of her being a little underweight, a tube of flea prevention drops and some yummy dog treats.

Yvonne and I were all set. We spoke about how lovely the website seemed, and how excited my mum would be that I had found a dog so soon. I did say I was a little taken aback by how rude the breeder seemed on the phone, but I thought perhaps she was just having a bad day or was sick of people messing her around. Yvonne laughed and said she thought it was probably just me being oversensitive, as per usual. If Yvonne doesn't like someone she will always just be upfront and say so. With me, I tend to want to try and see the best in people, and often get burned doing so.

On that journey down I also told Yvonne about the strange feelings of someone needing help that I had been getting in recent days, and that I just couldn't get any answers when I tried to find out where they were coming from. Yvonne replied in exactly the way that I had expected: 'All will show itself in good time. It always does.'

After munching our way through various family-sized chocolate sweet bags, a Little Chef breakfast and a few fizzy drinks, we were just a minute away from the address. We watched the sat nav carefully as it took us deep into a valley, then up a hill and along a beautiful country road, passing some stunning cottages covered in roses and other flowers lifting their heads up to the sun, which was streaming down. My stomach was now starting to churn a little, but I thought it was simply to do with all the junk we had eaten on the way down.

We arrived at the gates, which stood before a drive on the left. To get to the house, we drove around a bend in the drive and down into the area in front of the house. As we turned the corner, the house came into full view and we were greeted by a rather ferocious-sounding German shepherd cross, attached by a chain to its small kennel. He barked and barked, yanking hard on the chain to get to our car.

We slowly approached the area where we could park and we started to notice the surroundings. The house itself was a beautiful old country house with leaded windows, but surrounding it were filthy rags, old scrap, bits of wood and, to our horror, loads of empty filthy cat litter trays, piles and piles of them.

Yvonne and I looked at each other as we pulled the car up beside another that was in the drive. To be honest, there was so much rubbish around it was actually hard to fit my car in. We saw a few cats wandering around. Then to our left we noticed a large run, which was also full of rubbish and old bits of wood. The run was made from mesh and had what looked like the remains of an old bonfire in the middle. To our amazement, two shivering lurchers lay on the ground, staring back at us.

My legs froze. I suddenly realised that my heart was being

pulled towards these dogs. I felt as if it was being tugged right out of my body. The first dog was cream in colour, and looking very much the worse for wear, with visible scars on her head. The second was a brindle blue colour and very slim. She looked a little younger than the first. The feelings of desperation and helplessness washed over me again, filling me with dread.

'Oh, my god, Yvonne. It's them!' I whispered.

'I feel sick. Let's go, quick. I don't want to see this,' Yvonne quietly replied.

I saw her eyes surveying the area, looking at the rubbish everywhere. We could see old rows of sheds and hear sounds of barking and whining coming from within. There were also empty home-made chicken houses, but no chickens, with piles and piles of old scrap abandoned around what would once have been a beautiful home.

The view from where we were parked was simply outstanding. You could see for miles across the valley over open fields. It was certainly a remote place, but beautiful all the same. Well, it had been, once upon a time. It certainly wasn't anything like what I had imagined from looking at the website. No, that had told the story of what a brilliant, caring breeder Hilary was, how the pups and dogs all grew up with the cats of the house, by the fire in comfort and their lives full of love. The site had looked amazing and so had the dogs, apart from looking a little sad. But what little we had seen already was rather different, and we hadn't even got out of the car! I noticed the small area just in front of the view and thought, No wonder it looked lovely. That was the view behind them when the photos of the dogs on the website were taken.

I glanced up into my mirror to see the back door of the house open. 'Too late, she's seen us,' I said to Yvonne. A tall lady, in her mid-forties, was standing staring at us, frozen to the spot in our car.

This was Hilary and she was, unusually for a breeder, quite well turned out. Now, I have nothing against breeders looking glam, of course not, but my friends who breed are normally so busy with their dogs – walking, feeding and caring for them, looking after the puppies – that the last thing on their minds is doing their hair or putting make-up on. But this woman had clean hair which was dyed a white blonde shade and perfectly styled on her head. She was wearing hot pink lipstick and her eyes were made up. She at least gave the same impression as the website. She looked glamorous!

Reluctantly, we opened the car doors, gave a friendly wave and walked up towards the house.

'Hi, Hilary. I'm Joanne and this is Yvonne, my friend.'

She never said a word as she ushered us into the house. The stench of pee and poo hit us both as we walked in through a kitchen which was completely covered in old soiled newspapers, some intact and some ripped to shreds. On the worktops sat a couple of breeds of cats. They all seemed in quite good condition, but both breeds are well known in the cat world for their hardiness. I tried to hold my breath, or at least not breathe in too much.

She led us past a tiny Yorkshire terrier who was jumping up my legs, trying desperately to be picked up. Hilary gave a swift shout and the little dog scarpered into a corner. As I looked into the corner, I could see some sort of small dome. My eyes were drawn to it as my brain told me exactly what it was, but my heart was wishing it out of my brain. The image became clear, and I could see it was a cat tray, unrecognisable to the naked eye. There was no litter in it. This was head to toe, inside and out and back to front filled with dried-up poop. Every inch was covered, and I mean covered.

I tried to avert my eyes as best I could and look forward whilst watching my step for any deposits that were on the floor. As I entered the next room through a small home-made wooden gate attached to either side of the kitchen units, I heard Yvonne gasp. She was being ushered to a long wooden table and promptly sat down at the side of me to my left. At this point I still hadn't seen what she had gasped at, but then she looked me right in the eye and did a side look for me to see. My heart nearly stopped. There on the cold tiled floor, lying on what looked like a poo-soiled rag, was an emaciated old lurcher. She looked as if she didn't have enough energy to lift her head.

I turned in horror to look at Yvonne and saw tears welling in her eyes. Mine too began to fill as Hilary asked if we would like coffee. Coffee! Never mind the bloody coffee, I thought to myself.

'Umm, no thanks. We have just had one,' I lied.

I kept looking at the bitch on the floor, desperately wanting to help, but something held me back. I knew I had to stay quiet, for now at least, but trust me when I tell you, readers, that I was in turmoil inside. Through every vein, every pulse, I wanted to grab that dog and run!

'Is this the bitch, Hilary?' I asked politely.

'Yep. She is needing to put a bit of weight on, but she's a great dog. A hundred pounds, yes?' she replied.

'Umm, yes.' I counted the notes for her and handed them over. To be honest, I would have paid anything for that dog, just to get her out of there. But a hundred pounds was what we had agreed and that is what I gave Hilary at the table. The next minute her mobile went off and she made her excuses and went out of the room to take the call.

'Oh, my god, Yvonne. Look at her. It's the worst case I have ever seen,' I gasped.

'Joanne, this is horrific. My worry is what else she has. If

I can, I will go out for a cigarette and try and have a look about. Watch my back for me,' Yvonne replied.

'Will do. But be careful,' I said.

Hilary came back into the room and as she sat down again, the bitch tried to stand up, shaking and wobbling. I moved my chair ready to catch her if she fell, but somehow she managed to stand, tottering her way across the floor. The state of this poor dog was clear. She had no meat left on her at all. She was just bones with skin covering her. And worse still, all down her left-hand side, along the length of her whole side, was an open burn wound. The skin was peeling off, with puss coming out, and it was red raw to the core. We could clearly see this was the result of lying in her own urine.

'Hilary! She's trying to eat the poo from the box,' I yelped, pointing to the bitch, who had by now wobbled her way over to one of the four poo-covered cat litter trays. She was eagerly trying to eat the contents.

'Ah, don't worry. Meat in, meat out. It's all the same!' Hilary replied.

Yvonne and I were in shock. Our eyes could not believe what they were seeing. I could only think about getting this dog to safety and wondering what other animals she had, and what condition they were in.

'So, do you have many animals here?' I asked casually, trying to look as if I hadn't noticed how bad things were.

'Yeah, a few. Need to get rid of them, though. I have three days to move. They have to go!' she snapped.

'Oh, so you are selling more. What have you got?' I asked.

I had just taken some money from my bank and so had about a thousand pounds on me. I don't normally have much cash with me, and it was half my mortgage money and some money I owed my dad. What was I thinking?! I couldn't afford to buy animals, and had only come down for one for my mum. And I had nowhere to put any others. But a feeling of utter love came over me and I couldn't just walk away, so I asked about the Yorkshire terrier, who was pleading for me to take her. Hilary refused point blank. She said she was going to use her for breeding and the fact she was so small meant she could take her with her when she moved.

Then suddenly, out of the blue, she started saying that she knew her rights, and that the RSPCA had made her a visit, but she didn't let them in, she knew she could refuse. I wondered why she would even be telling us this. After all I was only asking what animals she had for sale (though I could certainly see why the RSPCA should visit).

Hilary clicked her mobile phone on and turned it around for me and Yvonne to see. 'Just look at this. That was him when I purchased him, and this is him now. I gave him on loan and look how he came back.'

Yvonne and I gazed at the screen, not quite able to take

in the horror we were viewing. The picture showed an emaciated Arab horse. Well, I may be wrong, but I doubt it. That horse's weight loss was not down to anyone other than Hilary, if the dog before us was anything to go by. No wonder the RSPCA had been calling on her. I just hoped and prayed the horse was now safe.

'I've got to have a cigarette now. I'll just be outside the door,' Yvonne said quickly, struggling to hold back the tears. She winked at me, to make sure I knew she was going to try and get a quick look around.

Hilary looked really uncomfortable at the thought of Yvonne leaving us. It was as if she didn't want us anywhere out of her sight, and I couldn't help wondering what else she was hiding from us.

Yvonne stood up and swiftly walked out as I tried to keep chatting about the weather, the old house and why Hilary was leaving. The explanation was a vague one, something about her ex-husband kicking her out. She said he worked away and wanted the house back, but to be honest it all sounded fake.

She was boasting about how the locals called her the lady of the manor, how much money she made, the power she had and how amazing her days as a breeder in the UK had been. It was all about her. Whatever the truth, I wasn't really interested. For me, it was all about the animals now.

I pretended to be a friend, not because I would ever befriend anyone like this woman, but because she was more likely to tell me what else she had for sale if she thought I was OK and non-threatening. So I played along with it, all the time knowing Yvonne was outside having a good look around. During what seemed like an age but was probably only about five minutes, Hilary offered me three other dogs at two hundred and fifty pounds each. Without even questioning I said I would take them and find them new homes. That way it would ease the burden for her.

She began to get angry and told me about one of the dogs, a male lurcher which was about eighteen months old. She had purchased him from another breeder in Ireland, but because he reminded her of another old dog, she absolutely detested him. Her words were vicious as her face showed the signs of pure evil. I couldn't help but feel sorry for this young dog, which I was yet to meet. What had he ever done to her? Why would anyone be so cruel as to blame him for anything a past dog may or may not have done? It didn't sit right with me at all.

Then she told me about the two other bitches. I hoped they might be the two I had seen lying outside upon arrival at the house, but she said they were in the sheds and that she would fetch them. She immediately stood up, grabbed the old lurcher bitch under her arm and proceeded towards the back door. I panicked as I remembered Yvonne might get caught snooping, so I asked to pay for the dogs now to save time, and luckily she agreed. The money was handed over and the receipt signed. I had spent nearly a thousand pounds in less than ten minutes!

Yvonne appeared just as we were heading towards the door. Her face was as white as a sheet as she stared at me blankly, showing utter shock.

'Yvonne, open the car back door. Let's put this dog in. Hilary has sold me another three,' I said. Yvonne walked up to the door and never even reacted at the words 'another three'.

Hilary almost threw the bitch into the back of my car and she landed with a thump onto the bedding I had placed there for the trip.

'You can't keep my collar,' Hilary snapped and whipped off the lurcher collar the bitch had round her neck.

'Oh, it's OK. I have my own,' I lied. I was just thankful the bitch was safely in my car. Then Hilary disappeared down some steps out of sight, telling us to stay put.

'What the hell have you seen, Yvonne?' I asked, worried.

'You do not want to know, really you don't. Just get the dogs and let's get the hell out of here,' Yvonne said.

The next thing we saw was Hilary dragging a squealing young dog by a thin rope lead from the shed to my car.

Almost unable to stand through sheer terror, this poor dog was shaking so much his legs could barely hold him up. I scooped him to safety in my arms, whispering something like, 'You are safe now, little one. Stay calm now,' and placed him, still shaking like a leaf, in the car. My heart was pounding like it was going to burst from my chest. Within seconds the third bitch and then the fourth were dragged out and thrown into the car by Hilary. I slammed my door, terrified she would change her mind.

But then I saw the look on the faces of the two dogs that were staring at me through the wire of the run. My heart sank. I have never in all my years working with animals felt the pull of desperation as I felt it that day. I used my communication skills and sent an image to the two bitches of me coming back for them.

I turned to Hilary and said, 'Those two, what about them? Let me take them. It makes sense, really it does. I can find a home for them and it will save you time, money and effort trying to take them with you.' I was desperate for her to agree, knowing in my heart it was killing me to leave them behind.

'No,' she snapped. 'Those are my best breeding bitches. You cannot have them. I need them.'

'Name your price!' I called after her, as she waved us goodbye. It felt as if she was forcing us to leave the premises.

'I said no. They are not for sale,' she snapped.

I wasn't really sure how I would have found the money, to be honest. I had spent almost everything on the four dogs I had in the back of my car, but I knew I needed to find a way. I looked over at them as we reversed the car from the driveway and whispered to them, sending a telepathic message. 'I will be back for you. I will not leave you, I promise!'

We got out of the drive and headed down the road in utter silence. Not even the four dogs made a sound. Everyone in the car that day was in shock.

About fifteen minutes later, Yvonne started to look at the dogs, which were now huddled together, shaking and terrified, in the back of my car.

'It was terrible, Joanne.' She shook her head, unable to comprehend quite what she had seen.

'Tell me. I want to know. Please,' I said.

'There was a cat house at the back of the house with around nine pens, all filled with faeces, probably months old. There was no litter. The cats were pure-bred cats, but they were just skin and bone with heads. They looked like the walking dead. Every single one that I could see was in a terrible state, with their noses and eyes streaming, sneezing and looking starved. They all need to be put to sleep as soon as possible.'

Yvonne looked away from me and out of the window, trying not to show her emotions. It was obvious that what she had seen was utterly horrific. We both wondered what else was left behind but agreed our main priority would be to help the dogs we had with us and hope and pray for Hilary to change her mind about the ones we had left behind.

We arrived at my mum's house and I told Yvonne to stay in the car whilst I prepared my mum for what she was about to see. I walked up to her door as she opened it, smiling from ear to ear with excitement about her new dog. But then she saw my face and her smile changed instantly to alarm.

'Mum, I need to talk to you. Please, let's just have a chat,' I said, and ushered her back into the house and onto the couch.

'What on earth is wrong, Joanne?' she said, looking extremely worried at the sight of her daughter crying uncontrollably, unable to speak a word of sense.

I'm not sure if it was what we had witnessed or just sheer relief at getting the dogs out that made me break down in tears, but it all came flooding out in a huge wave of emotion. I explained the whole situation and asked her to prepare for what she was about to see. We would need towels and some water, so we could check each dog over in military style before taking them back to Scotland with me. My mum ran around the house, gathering everything we needed. Then she watched as we carried the dogs in, one by one, and sat them down on a towel each.

It was the first time we had actually got a good clear look at them. Each one had various sores on them and they were all very underweight. They stank and were riddled with what we assumed to be mites. The young dog and one of the bitches had no fur left on their ears and they had urine burns and stains all over them. The old emaciated bitch looked in really bad shape. I even wondered if she could survive the journey back home.

Eventually, after all the dogs had been cleaned up as best we could, we decided that one of the bitches, who was totally shut off to the world around her, showing no emotion, would stay with Mum. She had, to my eyes, just given up. She seemed to have no will to live. She was showing no emotion, and wouldn't eat or drink. We felt she might find it easier to be with my mum, who is quiet and kind.

Yvonne and I both thought the emaciated bitch would need urgent veterinary treatment and round-the-clock care, and so was not suitable for my mum at this time. Yvonne agreed to take her on and I was to take the other dog and bitch until suitable homes could be found. We also agreed there and then that every dog needed a brand-new name as it was a new start. Without even looking at the names on my receipt book, I gave each bitch a pretty new name and the little dog a handsome one, because he was actually beautiful, with kind eyes and a heart so desperate for some love and affection.

It was late evening by now and we had to get the remaining dogs back to Scotland so we could get some veterinary help first thing in the morning. Yvonne took the old bitch to her house and I took the other two to mine, where they slept the night in a cage on a quilt in my kitchen. You would have thought I had given them a room in a five-star hotel the way they looked at that soft bed. The emotion was overwhelming.

The morning came, and Mum phoned to say her dog was coming round fine. He had taken a little food from her hand, but would not drink or go near food bowls, which we found a little odd. We had found the same issue with the others as well.

All the dogs were taken straight to the surgery and the various vets made out reports on each one. I arranged to get my two spayed and neutered later that week. Yvonne was told to give her old bitch plenty of TLC and the usual course of treatment for dealing with a dog in her condition.

I drove home feeling much more positive. I was ready to call the RSPCA to report Hilary now that we had photo-graphic evidence of all the dogs' conditions and treatment. But before I even got to my phone I heard it ring. Picking it up, I was surprised to see Hilary's number.

'Joanne, I've changed my mind. Come and get them,' she snapped in her usual nasty way. 'You'll need to be here by three o'clock as I am leaving today.'

I was a little taken aback. I had so desperately wanted to save the two bitches I had seen. And now, thank god, she had changed her mind.

'See you later. I will be there!' I replied without hesitation.

Yvonne and I didn't waste a moment. Ready for a ten- to twelve-hour round trip, we headed down the A1 like a bat out of hell, arriving at the house at around two thirty.

The scene was even worse than the last time. A strange, gaunt-looking bearded man seemed slightly startled by the car suddenly driving into the yard. He stood and stared at us both. We hadn't seen him before, but he took one look and turned around, dragging behind him what can only be described as a huge cement bag of something heavy. To both of us, it looked like something was dead in there. It could have been one thing or many, but whatever it was, he didn't wish us to see and scuttled off in the opposite direction, away from us.

I smiled at the two bitches, who were wagging their tails nervously at me. I just knew they knew they were being rescued. Call it intuition, call it gut feeling, but my heart was bouncing with a mixture of excitement and joy.

Hilary appeared at the door in no time and almost pushed

us in out of sight. The place was stripped of everything, but we noticed there were huge bluebottles buzzing around everywhere. There were at least a few hundred of them. They hadn't been there before, so why now?

Yvonne whispered to me, 'You know what that indicates, don't you?'

'No. What?' I replied.

'Death. Dead bodies!' she said quietly.

'Shush, Yvonne. I don't wish to know,' I said, trying to keep Hilary from hearing.

'I'm serious! Let's hope it was those poor cats in the bag outside, their suffering over, once and for all,' Yvonne replied.

'Money. Have you got it?' Hilary snapped.

I handed over the last of my money for the two bitches and she signed the receipt.

'What's happened to all your cats, Hilary?' Yvonne asked.

'Gone, gone to a friend's. She's keeping them all in the woods,' came her reply.

'In the woods? What do you mean?' Yvonne asked.

'She is a fellow breeder and exhibitor. She has them. Now go. I've got to get out of this place,' Hilary said, almost pushing us out of the door.

Within second the dogs were in my car and we were driving away for the last time. We headed straight for the local police station with the two dogs in the back of the car.

'Hi, I would like to report a cruelty case, please,' I said to the officer on the front desk.

'Are you saying it's happening right now?' she asked.

I explained the whole situation and what we had found. To my amazement, I was told to phone the RSPCA as it wasn't the police's business to get involved.

To say I fought my ground is an understatement. In fact, Yvonne almost had to drag me out in defeat before I got arrested myself! I could not believe they weren't interested in what was going on. I even explained that Hilary was about to leave the premises, and who knew what she would leave behind to die. Could they at least go down and check that no animals had been left? But the answer was still no. Unless a crime had been committed, it was not their job. I was furious.

We got back into the car and immediately reported the whole incident to the RSPCA. I also phoned one of Hilary's neighbours to tell them what was happening and ask if they could check the property for animals once Hilary had left. I was surprised to hear that they had been just as concerned as we were about what was going on at the house, but hadn't been able to get down to see. But they assured me they would check out all the sheds before nightfall.

Yvonne and I had done everything we possibly could and now we needed to concentrate on getting the lurchers back to health and into new loving forever homes. I had four lurchers at home and my two dogs, and Yvonne had the old bitch and her dogs. One by one, as the days and weeks went by, all the dogs were doing great. Whatever needed to be done was done for them and my students at workshops helped us raise money for veterinary treatment. My total outgoing bill was now well over two thousand pounds, so any help was gratefully appreciated. We hope the RSPCA did what they had to do, and pray nothing else suffered.

As fellow cat and dog exhibitors, both Yvonne and I asked ourselves the same questions. If we were breeders – which we are not – would we have felt comfortable with Hilary if she came to us and asked to buy a kitten or puppy for her breeding programme? Or if we had met her at a show and knew some of her best cats (we are not talking about the ones outside in the pens), would we have trusted her with one of ours?

Knowing how she looked and what a good impression her website gave, and having heard the stories she told about her lifestyle and how wonderfully she cared for her animals, we both answered that we probably would have been taken in. What a scary thought. So many breeders, so-called friends who have never set foot on her premises, have probably fallen for her lines. Many breeds of cats and dogs will have been sent to her and subjected to a life of hell.

And worse still, after doing some investigations of our own, we later found out where she had gone when she moved. Even though she has tried to hide it, she has now probably started up again.

I urge fellow exhibitors to home check, even when you think you know the breeder. Do it, and take no chances. Hilary managed to stay under the radar for so long because the lurchers she bred were never registered with the Kennel Club and were sold cheaply through the local paper. So too were many of her ill cats and kittens. Only a handful of good-quality cats and dogs were kept for the show ring. They helped throw a veil of secrecy over what was actually going on behind the scenes.

Scrolling through old Internet adverts, we found she had been selling many desired cross-breeds, such as puggles (pug x beagle), maltipoos (Maltese terrier x poodle) and so on. She would have needed to purchase the initial breeding stock from somewhere. It truly makes my blood boil to know that there are probably other people just like her out there in the UK, doing exactly the same thing as I write this. Breeding good-quality animals, promoting health and well-being, is fine, but it is our job as a nation of so-called animal lovers to find and help prosecute the rogue traders such as Hilary.

You may be wondering what happened to our rescue lurchers. Well, the good news is that the little old bitch Yvonne took home began to look great. All her sores healed, she put on weight and was really enjoying life. She was like a different dog. However, one morning she suffered a major blood clot in her spinal area and was permanently paralysed in all four legs. The hard decision was made to have her euthanised. Although she wasn't with us for long, it is good to know that her last days were spent happily. She was so close to death's door at the beginning, but pulled through so bravely. We will never forget her.

My mum's dog has come on in leaps and bounds. Eventually she began to wake up from the living coma she seemed to be in and started to enjoy life again, sniffing the air, chasing leaves and sticking to my mum like glue. She still has a long way to go, but she is slowly becoming a wonderful little companion. Last week she even went to stay with my sister Janice and her two children, Shannon and Billy, something that this dog wouldn't have been able to cope with before. Time heals and so will she. She is just gorgeous and my mum adores her.

The little dog turned out to be the most loving, delicate, funny little man, giving his all for a cuddle in the arms of his new family who love him.

And the other bitch, who had serious fear issues, has taken months and months to get to a stage where she can trust even a little bit. For now she is staying with me and we are nowhere near where we wish to be with her, but by the time you read this she will be in the hearts of a new loving family.

And last but not least, the two beautiful bitches I collected on the second trip both found lovely forever homes, and are doing amazingly well with their new-found families.

All in all, even though it was and still is one of those memories that hurts badly, it was the most rewarding time. I would like to thank everyone who helped both Yvonne and me with the financial support for the care of the lurchers. Thank you from the bottom of our hearts.

Here is a poem dedicated to the memory of Lady, Yvonne's little lurcher.

We all loved you, dear Lady, our furry friend.
We loved everything about you and always will.
May you take all the healing we could have given you,
release all resistance and attachment from here on,
and move happily into your new spiritual world.
Now we kiss you goodbye,
with love in our hearts
and light in our souls.
From this moment and for ever more
we offer you peace, strength and love.
Goodbye, our true friend Lady, goodbye.

We can all make a difference to dogs in need.

Chapter Five

Sometimes we need to take a look at the dynamics of our relationship with our animals. What we might initially assume is our pet's problem may well in fact be our own issue. Our pets might be absolutely happy within themselves, but we humans tend to strive for perfection and, in some cases, we might expect far too much from our animals. Sometimes the problem lies with the owner and not the animal after all.

I first met Charlie about two years ago. He is a huge jet-black standard poodle with an appetite for life like no other. Charlie is so happy all the time and just loves life.

His favourite time was meeting his owner's grandchildren at the school gates. They would wait with the mums for the school bell, and when the children came out Charlie would spin around in circles with excitement because he was so happy. The problem was, his owner couldn't get him to stop.

All of a sudden, at the sound of the children's footsteps and laughter, Charlie turned into a type of spinning top, whizzing round and round like a dog who is trying to catch its own tail but even faster and with more gusto. And Charlie isn't exactly a small dog, so he could easily knock people over with his exuberance.

Now any unfortunate child that happened to get too close to Charlie as they ran to their mother would be caught in this rush of excitement and whizzed around like a candy floss stick before being catapulted off at full speed, hopefully in the direction of the approaching parent! But not before Charlie had given them a big wet kiss, like a seal of approval that he was ready for the next one to join him. The children thought this was hilarious and the bravest would try and run past Charlie, secretly hoping they too would get caught up in the dog's spin. It became some sort of challenge to them at the school gates.

Whilst the other parents thought it quite amusing, Charlie's owner found the whole thing very embarrassing and spent most mornings apologising for her dog's lack of sanity. She just wished Charlie would be normal and stand still and greet the children as other big friendly dogs did and not turn into a raving lunatic, so she called me in to ask for my help.

I'd not come across an issue like this before. Charlie was a good dog and loved the children, so we weren't talking about a dog that was potentially dangerous, or a dog that the children were scared of. No, everyone loved him and his antics. So I felt a compromise would need to be worked out here. I didn't want to take away his character – after all this was why everyone loved him – but I needed to tone it down a little.

'Hi, Charlie, my name is Joanne,' I said, introducing myself.

'Hello, have you come to play?' he immediately asked.

'No, I have come to talk to you about the school trip you do every day with your owner,' I said.

'Oh, I love the school,' he replied, all happy with himself.

'Yes, I have heard you do,' I said. 'You get quite excited, don't you?'

'Of course! They laugh. I like laughing. Don't you?' he asked.

'Is this why you do your spinning at the gate?' I asked, smiling.

'They laugh, I laugh, we all laugh,' he replied happily.

'Charlie, your owner would like you to slow it down a little. Perhaps just wag your tail instead. Do you think you could do this?' Charlie had a full-size tail, unlike some poodles who have had their tails docked at a few days old (a practice which is now illegal in the UK).

'But this is my job!' Charlie replied.

'Your job?' I said.

'Yes. When I was young, my owner said my job was to be a good boy and keep the children happy and laughing as they were a little sad, and that we were to play with them and cheer them up,' he replied.

'Well, would it be possible to alter the job role slightly, and just calm it down a little? The children are getting older and require a role model now. They need a dog they can look up to, one who greets them at the school gates happily but calmly, like the handsome dog you are. Do you think you could try this?' I asked, hoping he'd get what I meant.

'No more laughing, then?' he said.

'No, of course you can laugh. It's just you are more grown up now and so are they, so laughing in a different way. I would like you to greet them with the wiggliest of tails. How about that?' I asked. 'And in return for your good behaviour, your owner says the children will play spinning with you when you get home.'

'OK, I will try,' he said.

I explained to his owner that we were going to compromise. The spinning was only to be done at home straight after school and he would try and stay calm at the school gates for her.

The next week she was delighted to report back to me that Charlie did indeed calm down. After just a few days the spinning had almost completely gone, although there were the few odd occasions when the children were overexcited and he forgot himself and burst into a spin. But he quickly managed to contain himself and after just a few circles he went swiftly back to huge wags of his tail. His owner kept her side of the bargain and each day after school the children took him into the garden and played ball, spinning and a host of other crazy games that made them all laugh. It was a happy ending for all.

'Morning, Joanne,' a friendly voice I recognised said to me one morning at my local supermarket.

'Oh, hello, Marion. You OK? And how's that lovely Benson of yours?' I asked.

Benson was Marion's pride and joy. A gorgeous Great Dane with the most fabulous temperament, he was a huge dog, standing the height of a small children's pony, and had a stunning white coat with a few odd patches of blue/grey colour. He was only three years old and adored everyone.

'Black!' she laughed.

'Black? What do you mean?' I asked, knowing he was an almost white dog.

'Please, Joanne, you must have a word with him. He is driving me and my husband around the bend. He is always black,' she giggled.

'But how? Why?' I asked.

'Well, as you know, he is pretty strong on the lead and so we rarely have him on one. Our grounds where we live are secluded, and it simply makes no sense. However, he has discovered the duck pond at the ridge,' she said, screwing up her face.

'Oh, the pond,' I giggled, knowing full well what Benson would do. (This was a huge pond at the bottom of their land, filled with a variety of wildlife from ducks to frogs, fish and a visiting heron. It was only about two feet deep.)

'Yes, well, as soon as I open the back door it's like he has a force pulling him down to the ridge. In he wades, chest deep in all the mud and slime, and plonks his bottom straight in. The problem is he will just sit there for hours on end, watching the birds or something, and we can't get him out!'

'Oh, so what do you do?' I asked, trying not to laugh as I had visions of this huge Great Dane stuck in the muddy water whilst both Marion and her husband, John, stood on the banks of the pond, trying their hardest to coax him out.

'Well, we've tried everything. My communication skills, which I learnt from you, food, bread with his favourite pâté, his boo-boo toy. But nothing will get him out. Poor old John even tried throwing a rope like a lasso to try and physically pull him out, but though he may be called John he is no John Wayne. He failed every time.' She sighed, grinning at the thought of her husband's attempts to be a cowboy. 'So we just have to wait and wait until he comes in himself. But – and it's a big but – when he does he is stinking! And black with mud. What can we do, Joanne? Any ideas?' she asked hopefully.

'Nope,' I laughed. 'He obviously likes it down there.' I was not being much help.

'Oh, come on, Joanne! You can do better than that. You are the psychic dog lady. Help me!' she said, laughing.

'Marion, this is what he loves to do. I'm afraid if none of his special toys or food can tempt him out, then you have to look at what you can do to make life easier for you, whilst still allowing him to be him,' I said.

'I don't get it,' she said, looking puzzled.

'Well, it makes him happy, doesn't it?' I asked.

'Yes, totally,' she replied.

'Well, we want him happy and if that is what floats his boat' (I laughed at the pun) 'then we don't really want to stop him enjoying himself. And he is in no danger. Look at it another way. He's coming to no harm, he's not chewing the house or being a nuisance. He is just taking himself off to enjoy nature,' I said.

'Yes, but . . . '

'Ahh, the stink . . . Now this is your issue – not what he is doing, just the end result. Yes?' I smiled.

'Actually, yes. It's not about what he is doing. If he wants to sit in the pond, that's fine by us. It's the stink and the mud we can't stand.' She laughed, grasping the point I was getting at.

'So it's about that, then, and that is simple to sort,' I smiled.

'Please do tell . . . I am all ears,' Marion laughed.

'Well, ask him to roll in the grass for at least five minutes when he gets out of the pond. Firstly, he will enjoy this, and secondly, the grass will clean him and dry him. It's fresh and will make him smell good too. That way he will be clean when he comes back in,' I explained.

'Genius! Thank you, Joanne. Why I didn't think of that I will never know,' she said excitedly.

A few weeks later I phoned Marion to see if her communication had worked with Benson and the pond situation, and she was thrilled. Instead of denying him his enjoyment, as so many of us would have done, she had told him to do it more. This had made him even more keen to please her and he had happily accepted her wish that he roll around on the grass to remove all the mud. A deal was struck that pleased everyone, and the problem was solved.

When you are having difficulties with your dog, always

think about what the real issue is and how you can compromise. Is it really about what your dogs are doing? Or is it something that is a result of what they are doing that offends you? Dogs deserve to have fun, so work out a solution that can make everyone happy.

'Joanne, my dog thinks he is a cat,' came the email.

Now this one intrigued me, because dogs really aren't as clever as cats. As a slave to cats I have the authority to say this. My five cats rule my house, so much so that Rosie and the family are completely under their control. Yes, *their* control. Cats are capable of determining what they want, need and require and unless you do as you are told they will make your life hell, so we slaves just get on with it. It is our job to serve.

Dogs, on the other hand, are happy whatever you do. They will wait, they will be happy if their food does not change, they are more than happy to work around your rules and your schedule. So why on earth would a dog think he was a cat? And why would the cats allow the dog to think this? I emailed for the full story.

It turned out that the family had four indoor cats: two Siamese sealpoints and two of mixed variety. The cats ruled the household (phew, not just me then after all) and so when the family took in a four-week-old pup who had been found abandoned, the puppy watched and learnt from the cats instead of mixing with other dogs and learning social skills from them.

Oddly enough, the cats took to the puppy and mothered him, constantly cleaning and washing him. They made him sit where they sat on a low windowsill, and soon he was jumping up and sleeping on a radiator bed and making noises at dinner time like a cat. The best of it was that this little pup was also using the cat tray to do his poops in!

Where's the problem, you may ask? Well, according to the owners this little pooch was now getting to be a big pooch. He was too big for a radiator bed and had fallen through at least two of them. He had a taste for jumping, and now he could jump up onto any work surface, not only the windowsill. And the litter tray was just not big enough. They would constantly hear it being crashed about as the oversized pup tried to squeeze himself in. They needed help!

The only option was to socialise the puppy with other dogs and allow him to rediscover who he was. He needed to learn that he was in fact a canine and not a feline, as he seemed to think. Much to the cats' disapproval, the owners invited a friend's small dog to come over on regular visits for a good few hours at a time, and arranged meetings with other owners and their dogs while out walking. The puppy soon got the hang of being a dog. It didn't take long, much to his owners' delight.

Soon the puppy was acting like a dog. He was sleeping in his own bed, going outside for his toilet breaks and barking instead of trying to make cat noises.

And the puppy's name? It was Felix. Yes, I know . . . It's a cat's name. Can't have everything, I suppose.

Butterscotch the Yorkshire terrier was a puppy with the heart of a lion. Not only brave but full of life, she was the little puppy in a litter of five that was said to have no chance of survival. She was disfigured when first born and her back legs were totally useless. Both the breeders and the vets decided she wouldn't have a good quality of life without the use of her back legs, and so the decision was made to have her put to sleep, much to my disapproval.

I begged them to allow me to take care of her and find her a home. This was something I felt was really important. There was nothing else wrong with her and my gut feeling was that she deserved the chance of survival, the chance of a home and the chance of life. And in the end they agreed.

During the time she was with me, I massaged her little legs every morning and every evening, to keep the circulation going. It soon became apparent that whilst they were not as well formed as the other pups', Butterscotch was gaining a little feeling in them and could push on them just enough to walk around on the carpet. The more I massaged the legs, the better they got. Granted, she was a little wobbly, but after a few short weeks she could run around and play with toys, which was incredibly heart-warming to me.

I never give up on dogs. I think they all deserve a chance of a happy life. That may mean putting in some effort at the beginning, but they are so worth it. Butterscotch came into my life about twenty-five years ago, and I learnt from her that anything is possible if you try. I will always remember her for that lesson.

Butterscotch was never going to be a show dog, nor was she ever going to walk as well as her litter sisters and brother, but she did bring her new owner unconditional love and lots of joy.

Here is an email about a common problem – but it's more of a problem for us than for our dogs.

> My dog is quite large and sleeps on my bed at night. The only problem is that now she takes up most of my bed. I end up with hardly any covers and, most of all, hardly any bed! Please help, Joanne!

Well, firstly, don't have the dog on the bed!

OK, I have to admit I am guilty of this too. I often wake during the early hours with only a corner of the quilt, my bottom sticking out and a rush of cold air on my back due to Rosie taking up the whole of the bed. Being a borzoi, she is huge and does fill most of the space. She spreads out and leaves me with a fraction of the bed. She dreams in her sleep and runs as if she is doing a marathon, kicking her legs into my back and making all sorts of noises, including snoring like a warthog! Not the ideal partner to have alongside you at night. I'd much prefer Mr George Clooney or Brad Pitt if I had the choice.

Rosie is often up on my bed and the truth is we all – OK, most of us – have the dogs up on our beds for a cuddle at some point. However, really and honestly, they should be given their own bed on the floor. Yes, I said it – on the floor.

Why? Well, firstly to prevent you from catching your death

of cold during the night whilst they are all wrapped up like a snug bug in a rug.

Secondly, so you can get a good night's sleep without the constant wiggling about and snoring noises coming from the dog. Thirdly, and most importantly, for safety reasons.

Safety? Well, dogs have dreams, just like humans. And in the same way as people can act out situations during their sleep, so too can dogs.

A friend of mine told me a story about her husband who was having a dream and thought they were in a car that was stuck. While his wife was happily sleeping, he got out of the bed, took hold of the bottom end and swiftly yanked the bed from the wall with all his strength, thus releasing the car which was, in his mind, stuck and in danger of becoming trapped with his wife inside. Only she wasn't inside any car. No, she was now in a heap on the floor, feeling bemused as the bed collapsed from under her. Her husband, still asleep, climbed back onto the broken bed and instantly drifted off again, leaving her in a state of dismay at what had just happened.

Now I know this is funny, but with dogs it can be quite serious. Whilst most dreams are harmless, I have heard about dogs fighting or defending themselves in their sleep whilst in a state of dream. This is very dangerous as you may just get in the way and the dog may attack you, causing serious harm, often to your face and neck area. Unfortunately, it does happen, so do yourself and your dog a favour and buy it a lovely soft bed to sleep in. That way it can still be with you in your room if you wish, but it and you are safe. Best of all, you can get your bed back!

Clients often ask me to ask their dogs to stop letting off raspberries. Sometimes this can be a simple request that I make to a dog, but sometimes the cause of the problem may be with the owner rather than the dog.

I met Kendal back in 2009. He was a mixed variety breed, standing about the size of a small coffee table, and had a rather large pointed nose and ears but a chubby body on shorter legs. He looked very healthy and had a gleaming black coat with a handsome white chest.

I was called in as Kendal was, according to his owner, 'doing things he shouldn't'. These things I soon learned were letting off raspberries or whatever you wish to call them – wind, trumps, pumps, blow-offs, trouser coughs. He was well known for doing this in front of guests, and they stank. My job was to stop him, and ask him to kindly do them elsewhere.

I arrived at the house, a huge manor house in Cumbria,

and Kendal greeted me. He was a lovely dog indeed. I sat down with his owner as he explained about his habit of letting off when guests were there. I listened carefully as the owner blamed the dog for his trumping episodes.

'What do you feed him?' I asked.

'Well, I don't think that matters. Could you just ask him to stop it?' the gentleman owner insisted.

I heard a small voice behind me saying, 'I can't.' I looked down and saw Kendal lying next to my bag on the floor.

'He can't,' I began.

'Well, how do you know he can't?' the gentleman asked.

'Because he has just told me he can't, so I have to listen to what he says,' I explained.

'Well, he has to, otherwise he is going to be moved outside,' the gentleman snapped.

'Tell him it's all his fault,' the dog started to say.

Oh, no. This was one of my worst fears. An argument was brewing between dog and owner. I had to nip this in the bud as soon as possible.

Since the man wouldn't tell me what he was feeding Kendal, I decided to visualise the feed bowl and offer it over to Kendal in my mind for him to telepathically fill up with his typical food. What I received back from this dog was a bowl full of what looked like chicken korma. Then I sent another bowl in my mind to Kendal and received back a similar picture of something that looked like a dark-coloured curry.

'I see you feed him on food that isn't real dog food,' I said.

'How did you know that? Did he tell you?' he asked, looking slightly shocked.

'Well, yes, sort of. He is showing me a curry-like food. Is this correct?'

The man began to blush a little as he explained that his wife had left him and he had been ordering takeaways, curries, fast food and pizzas for himself. Instead of buying dog food, he just ordered double of what he was having, for Kendal to eat. It was all this junk food that was giving the dog wind!

'Please buy some proper dog food of decent quality that's completely made for dogs. This will stop the wind Kendal is experiencing almost overnight,' I said.

'Oh, yes, of course. I hadn't realised. I thought it would be better for him, you know, with the fresh meat and everything,' he replied.

'No, a good dog food has everything Kendal needs, so let's stick to that and see how he goes,' I said, smiling. In the back of my mind I was wondering if the gentleman was suffering from the same problem.

'Thank you,' a small voice whispered.

'You are welcome, Kendal. Good luck,' I said, gently stroking his head.

A few weeks went by and eventually I received an email from Kendal's owner. It went like this:

> Greetings Joanne,
>
> The only raspberries in this house now are the ones I purchased yesterday from the shop. I am pleased to report Kendal and I are eating great. [At this point, I couldn't help thinking that maybe I had been right about his owner's wind too!]
>
> After your visit I went to the bookstore and purchased four books on natural feeding for dogs. I am now Kendal's personal chef of natural dog food, and whilst I make his I can prepare my own too. We are both feeling less bloated, with no more smelly wind and lots more energy. Thank you for solving the mystery.
>
> Regards,
>
> Mr J Turner

Well, this was a prime example of 'It's not the dog's fault'. Preventing wind isn't exactly rocket science, but just a simple case of giving your dog a decent diet.

If you are interested in feeding your dog the natural way, there are many good books on the market. Follow their suggestions carefully, making sure you provide all the vitamins and minerals that a dog needs. However, a decent dog food is just as good in most cases. Always go for the best money can buy. Remember, what goes in often comes out!

Kate is a friend of mine who had always wanted a dog but had never had one. So after the break-up of her marriage of eight years, Kate purchased a gorgeous little Westie called Jack. He was very cute, very lively and very, very naughty. So not really an ideal dog for a first-time owner. However, she loved him dearly.

Kate called me up one morning. 'Joanne, please help. He's done it again. I am sure he is doing it on purpose.'

'Doing what, Kate?' I asked.

'Peeing. You know – the little problem he has? I don't want him to hear me say he has a problem. He's sitting right beside me.' Kate was whispering into the phone, holding a hand over her mouth so Jack couldn't hear what she was saying.

'Kate, he will hear you,' I giggled. 'Jack is a dog. They speak in pictures and words, so he will telepath you. It's out – he heard you say he has a problem,' I teased.

'Oh, no! I don't wish him to know I think he has any problems. I don't, Joanne, really I don't,' she panicked.

'Too late, honey! The problem dog has been outed! And

anyway he has got a problem and you know it. That peeing business is out of control. So what's he done this time?' I asked, knowing full well that it wouldn't be anything normal like peeing on a carpet or up a lamp post.

'Oh, Joanne, he did it on purpose again. I was at the market yesterday when I met up with a friend of mine I hadn't seen in ages. She put her shopping bags down and we talked, but Jack kept barking at me to hurry up,' she began.

'Did he tell you that, Kate?' I teased again.

'Yes, he was telling me. You know he tells me all the time,' she said.

And actually I did know. This sweet little innocent dog was so demanding that he was a pain in the butt. Poor Kate spoilt him rotten and he took advantage of her, dictating everything. Whilst I am all for our pets asking or showing what they want, this little dog went to the extreme.

'So, what happened?' I asked.

'Well, I asked him to wait and I thought he had listened because he went blissfully silent. So we carried on chatting.'

'Well, that's good,' I replied, knowing full well there was more to come.

'No! He went silent because he was in the shopping bags. He was quietly eating half her shopping. And then, when we caught him, he looked straight at me and then at my friend and did a pee right in the bag with all the fresh fruit and vegetables in. And that was the only bag he hadn't eaten out of. I couldn't believe it!'

I found this whole incident funny but it really didn't surprise me at all. He had got into all sorts of trouble before, peeing inside a lady's handbag, pooping on a carpet at a market holder's stall, peeing up a man's leg at the post office and doing the same to a lady who was bending down, picking up some loose change that she had dropped. He only missed her head by a whisker, much to her horror.

'You really need to have more control of that wild animal of yours,' I laughed.

'It's not funny, Joanne,' she giggled.

'So what did you do?' I asked.

'I paid for all her shopping, that's what I did. Can you believe it?'

'Umm – of Jack? Yes!' I laughed.

'Help me. He has to stop it,' she said, containing her laughter. 'He is costing me a fortune.'

'OK, here's what you do. You have to be firmer with him. Keep him on a lead and never take your eye off him.'

'That's it?' she said.

'Well, for now, yes. And take him to some classes. He needs to start listening to you, to find out what's right and wrong, what's acceptable behaviour and what's not. But you need to carry this through at home too, Kate. It's a long-term commitment. You are the boss, not him, and once he realises this then you can become partners.'

'So everything you have already told me in the past, then?' she laughed.

'Yep, that's it. I'm not a miracle worker. This one is down to you, Kate.'

Sometimes with dogs it's your behaviour that needs to change first and this will come automatically if you become a leader. In Kate's case, Jack was the leader and so behaved badly and took advantage. It was down to Kate to do the famous actions of just enough love, lots of good old-fashioned language and plenty of leadership (I will tell you more about this in Chapter Seven).

I am happy to report to you readers that Kate is getting there slowly. Yes, Jack will always be naughty Jack, but at least he has stopped peeing on people and their bags.

Dogs are social animals, and on occasions they can develop jealousy issues. This may happen because there is a change in circumstances in their family life, with a new baby, new owner or new animal being introduced. It's common for people to panic a little and not understand how the dog is feeling. They may have given no thought to the effect these changes have actually had on the dog.

This is, in my opinion, an issue that should not be ignored. Jealousy can lead to bad behaviour, destructive actions and even aggression. Here is a story that I heard at a recent workshop.

Sandy the golden retriever, Julie and her husband, Ben, had all been living together quite happily for five years. When Julie found out she was pregnant she and Ben were delighted. And as Sandy had been the perfect dog for the last five years, they had no reason to think his behaviour would change when the baby came along. They were not prepared for what happened next.

The baby arrived and Sandy's behaviour changed dramatically, almost from day one. Whenever the baby cried, Sandy would start to growl. He hated the baby and was so jealous. On occasions it got so bad that he began shaking uncontrollably. He had to be placed in another room, well away from the baby, in order to be at a safe distance.

As we know, this is not the usual behaviour of golden retrievers. They are normally great family dogs. But it showed Julie and Ben that, no matter how much you think you know your dog, you have to be aware that a simple change like bringing a baby into the home can alter the dog's personality.

Julie was also an experienced communicator and she decided to work with Sandy, giving him lots of extra time, affection and one-on-one attention. The outcome was not what she had imagined. It turned out that Sandy just hated babies, and there was no getting around the fact. This was the reality. He didn't like their smell, their noise or their interference, as he called it, with his previously quiet home life.

Obviously, no chances can be taken in a situation like this. The baby's safety was paramount and a decision had to be made. Sandy was rehomed with Julie's mother. Luckily he was keen to go, as his life with Julie and Ben was no longer one he enjoyed.

Now this was an extreme, but the right decision was made for both the dog and the family. In some cases it just takes a little common sense. If your dog is used to being the centre of attention and then something changes that means he is pushed to one side, stop for a moment and think how this may affect him. Some animals will go into a deep depression, others start developing unusual behaviour patterns. It is important to invest some time with your dog. You need to reassure your dog that he or she is still loved, no matter what happens. This will nearly always banish the bad behaviour.

Never, ever leave children alone with dogs. Even the sweetest dog can still have a wild dog instinct and may attack in times of stress or jealousy. Dogs see biting or attacking with their teeth as protective measures, but this behaviour could lead to a life-and-death situation for the victim involved, and it may happen in a matter of minutes. Always remember that dogs can be dangerous, no matter what their shape, breed or size.

Be aware of what is going on with your dog at all times, watch for any changes in personality and, if you can, catch and deal with them as soon as possible.

Why is it that when we girls have a new boyfriend our calm, loving, cuddly little dog suddenly becomes a ferocious tiger determined to keep the two of you apart? Well, this is one of the most common problems that I come across with new lovers. And so I thought I'd share this email with you.

I have recently met a wonderful man, who is gentle, kind, loves animals and is everything that I have been looking for. So what's the problem, you may be asking? Well, it's my dog, Scamp. He is about twelve years old and just a small wire-haired mixed variety. His health is fine and in general he acts normally – that is until my new boyfriend comes around to see me. Then my precious little dog turns into a nightmare.

Scamp is usually really well behaved and he likes everyone, but he won't let me sit next to my boyfriend. He growls and stares at him. If my boyfriend even touches my arm or leg Scamp will leap up and attempt to bite him (thankfully he has few teeth left and so gum damage is the best he could do).

It's just really embarrassing. He won't take a telling off and my boyfriend thinks I have no control.

I replied that Scamp is scared of the new boyfriend taking his mum (or his partner or pack) away. He sees this man as a threat and so is defending his family. If you think about wild dogs, they live in a pack and they work hard to keep it harmonious and stable. When a threat such as an outsider comes along they will naturally see that threat off, thus securing their family. And that is all Scamp is trying to do.

The best move is to integrate the new boyfriend slowly. Start a bonding process, away from the house at first. Let him come with you when you take Scamp out for walks, let him give him treats, play ball or Scamp's other favourite pastimes, just allow him to edge in with no threat, so that he is not seen as taking anything away but becomes an enhancement to the relationship. Scamp will soon accept him and life will be back to normal again.

After just one week the owner emailed back saying Scamp was so much better and that the three of them were happy and enjoying time with each other. Scamp now sees the new boyfriend as a positive experience, not a negative, as they always do something fun when he is around.

Dogs can often become very protective when a new relationship starts, and there are various steps you can take to make a happy transition for all involved. It only takes a short while to turn a situation around, so put the effort in and be consistent. It is so worth it.

Firstly, get your partner to meet the dog in a neutral place, such as out on a walk in the park or on the beach. And get him or her to play with the dog so they can build a friendship. That way, the dog will actually like the new person you are bringing into your life.

Ask the new partner to bring the dog a little treat whenever they come to the house, or to give the dog some cheese from the fridge to help create a bond.

Giving the dog attention, taking it for walks and generally

just being around will build trust. If the dog can trust the new partner, then he or she will trust them around you.

Never tease your dog. I have seen people sit with their partners and find it rather funny to wind the dog up by kissing and cuddling, so that the dog, who is already jealous of the partner, starts to bite and growl. By doing this you will stress the dog out, and you can actually create a dangerous dog. Please treat your dog with respect and work hard to develop a good relationship with your partner and your animal.

Dogs are incredibly intuitive, sensitive, clever, funny and inquisitive. Oh yes, and in my personal experience they can be utterly embarrassing, too! Minti, my late poodle, was tiny, white and very cute, but with an attitude to match any larger dog.

I had just met my boyfriend of the time and I was all loved up, as you can imagine in the first weeks of romance. This particular evening, we had settled down to watch an old movie whilst sharing a lovely bottle of fine red wine and a huge bar of Dairy Milk chocolate. We were cuddled up on the couch, content with being in each other's arms, and Minti was lying right beside me.

I made my move to kiss my boyfriend and just as I leant

forward, blwuuubbb! Minti blew the loudest raspberry I have ever heard come from a dog's bottom. For a little dog, she could sure let one rip! I stopped about an inch away from my boyfriend's lips, eyes wide, frozen in shock, not really knowing whether to say sorry or not. And because Minti was lying right next to my own bottom, it sounded like it had come from me!

He just smiled and said, 'Never mind. Now give me that kiss,' but I couldn't. I was so embarrassed and spent the next ten minutes trying to explain it hadn't been me but the dog. Somehow, I don't think he ever did believe me. And I never got the opportunity to put my own good advice into action!

Just last week I was on the phone to a friend and we were discussing how intuitive dogs can be. I have known Cara for many years, since we were children to be exact, and we began to recall some memories of her old dog, Bonnie.

Bonnie was a cross beagle, with big floppy ears and a face that looked full of innocence. She was the colour of a beagle – white, black and tan – with the blackest of noses, and that nose could sniff out anything. I suppose that was only to be expected, since beagles are scent hounds, but we were not sure what else she was crossed with. She certainly must have got her stockiness from the other breed. Bonnie sported a big bottom and shortish legs.

She was a lovely, caring dog and very much Cara's best friend. So when Cara's new boyfriend Rob (now her husband) came along, Bonnie found it quite hard to adjust to the relationship. At the time she was only around six months old, and she would often growl and misbehave.

Rob was kind and did the usual nice things to win Bonnie round. He would bring her doggy chew sticks or feed her a little cheese every now and then. As Bonnie was still young and a typical puppy, food seemed to do the trick in helping her accept Rob as a welcome part of Cara's life. Eventually she allowed Rob to be a member of the family, although on occasions she still gave the odd snarl of the top lip to warn him away from Cara.

Then one day Bonnie began to act really strangely. She wanted to sit on Cara's knee all the time, which was something she had never wanted to do before. She would clamber clumsily up into her lap and press herself deep against her, giving her a cuddle like no other. This was kind of nice, but it could be a little uncomfortable at times, bearing in mind that Bonnie was growing rapidly each day. She was not exactly a small dog and she did weigh slightly too much to be a lapdog.

But what was becoming more noticeable was that every

day, first thing in the morning when Cara woke, Bonnie went straight to her. And when she did her lap sitting she would be really possessive, making sure no one else could get near to Cara. She stuck to her like glue, growling at anyone coming close, especially Rob.

Bonnie's behaviour was becoming a problem and Cara dealt with it by immediately placing her back on the floor as soon as she started to become possessive. But then she would start whining to get back up. This obsession to be on Cara's lap had come out of the blue and no one was quite sure why Bonnie's behaviour had changed.

And then, around three weeks later, Cara found out that she was pregnant with her first child, Emma. Rob and Cara were delighted with the news. But Bonnie had known before it was obvious to any of us. Cara said she had thought it was strange that Bonnie would nuzzle into her tummy with her nose, but she had thought nothing more of it. She laughs now, saying, 'Looking back, it was so obvious. I don't know why I never clicked. Bonnie was a great contraceptive pill as it was difficult for Rob to get near me when she was around, but in the end she was also the pregnancy predictor!'

This is not the first time I have heard stories like this. It is well known that dogs have amazing abilities when it comes to predicting what is going to happen. These instincts are so strong that even scientists find them remarkable.

Chapter Six

Many of the readings I do involve animals that have passed over. In fact, I would say that about ninety per cent of my readings in the last four years have been with animals that are in spirit. I was speaking about this not long ago with a good friend of mine who is also an Animal Communicator, and it turned out she was the complete opposite to me. Ninety per cent of all her readings were with living animals, whereas mine were with passed-over animals.

Why would this be? Well, I am not entirely sure. I think perhaps it is because I have experienced so many losses myself that I can relate to and understand just how hard it can be for the humans left behind.

If I ever doubted that there is more to an animal than its physical body, those doubts were laid to rest by my late poodle, who was eighteen years old when he passed to spirit. It was Mr Klein's appearance on my bed a few months after his death that completely validated my belief in the life of the spirit. It was as quick as lightning, but the glimmer of my Mr Klein, happy and well again, made my heart relight with the unconditional love he had shown me for those eighteen years. I knew he was at peace and it was as if he gave me the green light to let go of my grief and move on.

Even as a communicator, I am humbled by the mystery of life and death and beyond. 'Where do they go?' people often ask me. I have on many occasions asked the animals where they are or where they go to, but each time I do, the answer is swerved or they say it's not my time to know. We may call it Heaven. We may call it Rainbow Bridge. We may just call it the Universe. It doesn't really matter where they may be and if I am honest, I do not know. Truly, I have no idea.

I actually do not think anyone will ever know, not until we go ourselves. In my opinion, we are not meant to know. Not one human spirit or animal spirit whom I have had the pleasure of talking with has ever given me the answer. I know it's a lovely place, but where . . . ? That's the million dollar question!

Another question people often ask is 'How does it work?' I think of it as being a bit like the way I communicate with clients from all over the world on the Internet. Today's wireless communication means that my work can reach thousands of people from around the globe easily, and this is similar to talking with animals that have passed over to the spirit world.

Now, you might wonder why I would say this, but let's

think about it for a moment. I type a message to a client from a faraway country and then I hit the send button with my message attached. Somehow, my message gets through. There are no wires connecting us. The message travels through empty space. And, within minutes, I receive a 'Hello' and a message back. It's just the same as connecting with an animal that has passed over.

One thing is for sure, no matter what the distance between us, animals can and do communicate easily with us from the other side. We all continue to have a connection with them, just as we do with our loved ones that we have lost.

I had been working with a lady in America called Hannah, who contacted me about the family dog, Elsie. A pure-bred Maltese terrier, Elsie was a little white ball of fluff. She was no taller than a tin of Quality Street, with really short legs and a very cute face, full of mischievousness, and the blackest of noses that was always pointing in the air like she was a tiny drama queen.

Hannah had contacted me because Elsie had a habit that was driving the family mad. No amount of training would get her out of it, and they were beginning to think there might be something seriously wrong with her. When I asked what the problem was, Hannah explained that, at the same time every afternoon, Elsie would stand in the same spot looking into the corner of the room. She would just stare at a blank wall, not moving an inch. They couldn't move her, and if they did, she would wriggle out of their arms and instantly return to the same spot. This behaviour was happening every day without fail, and would last for exactly forty-two minutes. They were baffled and had decided to see if I could find out what she was doing.

I asked to see a photo of Elsie, which Hannah sent through to me via the Internet and boy, was she cute! I think even the toughest dog owner (you know, the ones that love big, scary-looking breeds) would melt when they saw her. She was lovely. In the photo, her white hair was neatly tied up from her face so she could see and positioned in a topknot sporting a bright pink bow.

She looked like the most pampered little dog, lying on a pink purpose-made cushion, which had gold beading sewn around the edge and the word Elsie embroidered on the pink velvet cover. She looked every bit the princess, with her coat trimmed to perfection in a sort of puppy trim. This isn't something Maltese people often do with their coats, but I have to say Elsie really did suit the look.

I felt an instant connection when I tuned into her photograph. The way this normally happens is that my heart feels as if it is opening up, like a flower in the morning sun. I always get a slight tingly feeling in my hands and fingers and I feel a complete connection pulling me into the picture. Elsie was eager to chat and I was pleased to do so too.

I made my introductions and asked some simple questions, such as what she liked to eat and where were her favourite places. I do this so that the dog gets to understand I am not a threat, and actually here to help, whether they need it at the time of communication or at any time in the future. I like to let them know that I will be there for them, just in case they need me.

Before long I was able to start finding out why Elsie was staring at the wall.

'Elsie, is there something you do every day at a certain time?' I asked, trying to think of a way of putting it across.

'Yes,' came back her reply.

Bingo! I thought to myself. That was quick. She's going to tell me.

'I eat every day at the same time,' Elsie said happily.

Oh no, this wasn't what I was after. So I tried again. 'No, Elsie. Something else, something that you do and it takes exactly forty-two minutes?'

'Oh, Alfie,' she said, as if I should already know.

'Alfie?' I questioned. I wasn't sure what this had to do with her behaviour.

'Alfie, my brother! I meet him,' she replied.

Now I wasn't aware of any other dog in the house, as Hannah had said Elsie was their only dog, so I was a little confused.

'So, tell me more about Alfie, Elsie,' I said, hoping she could give me a little more information.

'Well, Mama thinks he's gone, but I show her he hasn't. He's with us every day,' she replied happily.

'Alfie? Alfie's with you every day? So tell me again, Elsie. Who is Alfie?' I asked.

'Alfie comes to see us. He likes to come,' she replied.

'From where, Elsie?' I asked.

'From spirit. He comes in every day. He doesn't have much time, but he likes to come back. Look,' she replied.

As she stopped talking, an image of another dog came straight into my mind. He was the same breed as Elsie, a Maltese, but slightly bigger and his coat was long and flowing. Instead of one topknot, he had two, one either side of his head, neatly tied with blue plastic-looking bands. I looked at the image in my mind and instantly heard the words, 'Tell her I'm OK, please.'

'Hello, is that Elsie?' I asked.

'No, I'm Alfie. Could you tell her I'm OK, please, my mum? I'm here every day,' he repeated.

'Of course I can,' I replied.

'She says she misses me every day, so that's why I come back every day,' he said.

I felt a gush of love through my heart and promised I would tell his mum, Hannah. I thanked both dogs and phoned Hannah straightaway with the results of the reading.

'Hannah, Elsie is seeing another dog. His name is Alfie. Right?' I asked.

The phone went quiet for a moment and I could hear sniffles down the line.

'Are you OK?' I asked her.

'Yes, sorry. I knew it was him. I just felt stupid telling anyone. I had that feeling that he had come back to me. Just yesterday I thought I saw him, but I put it down to my imagination!' she cried.

'Well, this is what happened when I connected with Elsie,' I said, and I told her the whole story of what Elsie had relayed to me about Alfie visiting. 'Hannah, when did you have Alfie? You never mentioned him,' I asked.

'Joanne, I spent seven years with both the dogs, brother and sister,' she began.

'Yes, that's what Elsie said. That he was her brother. He was handsome, too, wasn't he?' I said.

'Very. He used to wear his hair—'

'In two topknots, not one?' I interrupted.

'How did you know that?' she asked excitedly.

'Well, he came through clear as day to me, Hannah. This doesn't happen all the time, but he so much wanted to send you his love. Your connection is so strong together, still,' I said. Allowing the animals to pass over their personal messages of love and warmth to their owners is so important to me, and it helps the owners so much.

'Yes, he was a very special dog. I miss him all the time and tell him every day,' she said.

'I know that, too. I think it's about time you let him go. He's ready, Hannah, and I think once he goes, Elsie will stop her behaviour. She is just seeing what you perhaps can't,' I said, hoping she would allow me to help her release Alfie's spirit.

'Of course, Joanne. How selfish am I? I couldn't let him go!'

'You can now. You know he loves you and always will. Now, tell him tonight when you are relaxing that it's time to release to spirit,' I explained to her.

Hannah agreed and later that evening she released Alfie to the world of spirit. From that day forward Elsie never sat staring at the wall again. Alfie had gone with everyone's blessing, leaving behind a heart full of fond memories.

Our own animals often have a connection with passed-over

pets, and it is not uncommon for me to deal with clients who are convinced their dogs see or sense spirit ('spirit' here meaning people or animals that have passed over to the other side).

In 2010 a couple called Howard and Sally Blake contacted me for a reading for their beloved dog Baxter. He was a beautiful Weimaraner with a short, dense, blue to silver-grey coat. His eyes were so very soulful. Male Weimaraners are large, at 25–27 inches at the shoulder, and weigh 65–85 pounds, and Baxter was no exception. He was a very handsome, well-built boy and his family loved him so much.

When Baxter passed over to spirit Howard and Sally found the weeks after his death really hard to deal with. The grief of losing such an amazing dog, companion and friend was almost too much to bear, and so they called me to see if I could connect with him through my readings. They wanted to make sure he was happy and to have the comfort of knowing he was safe.

Baxter was an easy dog to contact through communication. He was social, happy and keen to let his owners know he was OK. They had blamed themselves for not being with him at the vet's when he had passed over, but the truth was that Baxter didn't hold a single grudge. In fact, he asked me quite clearly to tell them he was fine, he was going to go to spirit no matter what the vet tried to do and they were not meant to worry or hold on to any guilt whatsoever. It was his time to cross over. He also showed me various pictures of himself in the spirit world with an older gentleman and another dog, the same as himself.

I passed all this information to Howard and Sally, not knowing that Howard's mum, who is psychic too, had received exactly the same information. My reading and her reading completely validated life after death for Howard and Sally, and so they were finally able to come to terms with Baxter passing over, knowing he was safe and well in the spirit world. Here is the note Howard sent to me:

Hi Joanne,

I thought I would just let you know that following your incredible letter about our beloved Weimaraner Baxter, my mum, who has always seemed to be a little psychic, had a clear message yesterday from my grandmother's brother, my Great Uncle Ken, who died in 2003. He, as you completely described in your letter, was a tall man, always smartly dressed. He was a river keeper in nearby

Eastleigh. He loved dogs and had a Weimaraner too, which you mentioned! We don't know the dog's name, though! The message to my mum was very clear and has scared her a little. Uncle Ken's voice said, 'Gilly, tell your boy not to worry, I got his dog!'

Mum told me rather shakily on the phone yesterday and was debating whether to tell me or not but I'm so glad she did. It completely validated your reading, not that we needed it!

I can't tell you how happy your letter and this message has made both Sally and me!

Thought you'd like to know!

Best wishes

Howard and Sally x

I find it hard to describe how I feel when a client gets his or her validation that their dog is indeed absolutely fine on the other side of life. I can only say that I have shed many tears of joy with my clients on such occasions. I know how hard it is to lose a loved dog, and being able to give some sort of validation and closure has got to be one of the most rewarding parts of my work. As upsetting as it can be, I wouldn't change it for the world.

When I have spoken with animals who have passed into the spirit world, they are often with family members. Funnily enough, these are sometimes members of the family who weren't really close to animals in their lives!

A few years back I held an Animal Communication workshop where something happened that I will never forget.

It was a Sunday in late June and I had about twenty-five people in the room. We had several animals booked to join us for the day and the students and I were all keen to meet them. An hour in and I had done the usual introductions – who I am, what communication means to me and how they too would be able to use communication by the end of the day – when out of the corner of my eye I noticed a small white flash. It was weaving in and out of the chairs, trying not to draw attention.

I carried on with my presentation, whilst all the while the little white flash kept whizzing around the room without anyone seeing it but me. The more I tried to concentrate on what I was supposed to be saying, the clearer the image got. What had at first seemed like a shady white area moving around now slowly became a small dog shape. It was a little white dog. I still couldn't work out the exact breed but it was no bigger than a footstool.

Around it whizzed as I talked, but now I could clearly see

what it was doing. The students had their belongings, such as bags, pens and papers, by their chairs. This little white dog was running around and sticking his nose into each bag. This suddenly got my attention as one lady leant down at the exact moment the dog's nose was in her open handbag, almost as if she could feel a presence.

'Are you OK, Barbara?' I asked, smiling.

'Umm, yes. Sorry, I thought I . . .' And with that she stopped what she was saying.

'Please, tell me. It's important,' I replied, giving her a nod of encouragement.

'No, it's nothing. I just thought I heard – no, felt – Sam, my old poodle, next to me,' she said, dropping her head and looking a little embarrassed. 'But he died a few years back. Sorry, Joanne. Sorry, everyone. It must be this course making me all emotional.'

'Not at all,' I replied, now seeing this little dog completely.

I decided to show the students that animals do live on and, not only that, they still do what they did best when they were living. In this little dog's case it was sticking his nose into handbags!

'Barbara,' I said, 'let me give you the validation you are waiting for, honey. Your dog was a lovely little white poodle. His coat was – well, what he is showing me now is a special trim, unlike most pet poodles you see. He has four white pompoms on his ankles, a pom on his head and tail, and his body is trimmed to about an inch all over. He has a nose for food and, just like my little poodle Mr Klein who I lost to the spirit world, he adores chicken. Now, four of you ladies here today have chicken sandwiches in your bags.' I laughed, pointing at the second lady to my left, the sixth lady, the nineteenth lady to the right and indeed Barbara herself. 'I'm right, aren't I?' I said, grinning.

The class was now laughing, as the four ladies I had chosen picked up their sandwiches from their bags to reveal chicken fillings of various descriptions.

'Bloody hell, Joanne is psychic!' the only gentleman of the group laughed, to the delight of the ladies.

'Well, yes. But do you want to know how I know?' I asked them, grinning.

Barbara started to giggle. 'I know how you know, Joanne, but do tell them anyway.'

'Well, this little spirit dog has spent the last fifteen minutes going from bag to bag, focusing his efforts on your four handbags. He has been running from one to another, sticking his nose right in and wagging his pom on his tail like some sort of gundog flushing out game from tall grass,' I said. 'He's so funny, Barbara, and reminds me so much of my Mr Klein, who could sniff out a piece of chicken from a mile away!'

The room fell about laughing and Barbara was overjoyed that her dog Sam was indeed fine and up to his old tricks. 'He really loved chicken sandwiches, Joanne, above all else. We used to go on picnics and I always brought him chicken sandwiches.'

Barbara was so happy that he had joined her at the workshop that day. She felt that she could now move on and take comfort in remembering Sam and all his funny little quirks.

Now you may laugh at this possibility, but in my work as an Animal Communicator I have found that it is quite common for some animals that have passed over to the spirit world to play out past lives, just like Sam the poodle. This is often referred to as residual energy, meaning it's a playback in time.

And some animals will actually come back permanently. By this I do indeed mean reincarnation. Yes, over my years of working in the field of Animal Communication, I have actually experienced this with various animals.

I had heard when I was young that humans are capable of such a thing. Having listened to various people who believed a hundred per cent that they were from a past life, I read many books on the subject, including some about children under the age of five. They were able to say who they thought they were and where they had been in a previous life, give their family name and talk about their brothers and sisters, among other things. When independent journalists looked into the actual details, there was no denying that what the children had told them was true and the various facts could indeed be validated.

The fascinating details for me were the distances involved. Some of these children were describing places which were hundreds and in some cases thousands of miles away! Now, whilst you might say an adult could have read up on the information, there is no way a child who could barely read or write would have been able to describe the facts to such a perfect degree of validation.

So these were my first experiences of reincarnation and the mystery behind it all. Yes, the human side of it had me convinced, but I had never heard about animals coming back until I experienced it myself through my work.

Many years ago now, I did a reading of a black Labrador called Taylor. He was a very wise-looking two-year-old. His owners, Kevin and Marie, said that he was almost identical to a dog they had owned many years before, when they first got married.

Kevin and Marie simply wanted to be sure that Taylor was happy with his life and living conditions. The only purpose of the reading was to make sure he was OK. But I was about to find out something I wasn't expecting at all.

I began with my usual introduction of who I was, and why his owners had asked me to make contact with him. I encouraged him to chat to me as a friend, so that I could pass on any messages that he wanted to send to Kevin and Marie. And then he totally shocked me with what he said.

'Tell my dad, Kevin, it's me. I'm back,' Taylor said.

'Taylor, why do you say "back"? What do you mean?' I asked.

'They call me Taylor, but I am London,' he said.

'London? What do you mean? You come from London? Is that where they got you?' I asked, thinking perhaps this was a validation answer for his mum and dad, something that would validate the reading.

'No, I am London,' he said. 'It's me. I've come back to them.'

I realised that it wasn't the City of London he was talking about, as I had assumed to start with (first rule of communication – never assume!) but that his name was London. So why did they call him Taylor? I wondered to myself.

'I have come back. I had the chance and I took it. My name

183

is London. Tell them I'm back,' he kept insisting over and over, as if to make me really listen.

'Yes, I will. So you were called London in your last home?' I questioned, thinking that perhaps he had been renamed.

'No, I have come back, not renamed,' he said, as if reading my mind.

I began to think about the reincarnation stories I had read and decided I'd ask him. Whilst it was a long shot, it seemed the only explanation for what he was trying to get across to me.

'So you have been here before? As another dog?' I asked a little nervously.

'At last! Yes, I was London before, the time before,' he began. 'Tell them it's me. I came back. I got the chance and I took it.'

'Who gave you the chance?' I asked him.

'Them. Not sure. Just said I could come back, as I missed them so much,' he replied.

'Where were you then? And how long have you been away?' I asked, hoping I would get some sort of clear answer.

'Just around. It was nice. Saw lots of friends. And not long, no. Hasn't seemed to be long,' he said, sounding slightly confused.

'So, do you know where you were exactly?' I asked again.

'Not really, but it was nice. I was happy, but I missed them. I'm with them, you know, in the picture,' he said.

'What picture?'

'The three of us, special picture. I was dressed like him,' he said.

I was now losing what he was on about. Why would a dog be dressed? And like who?

'Who were you dressed like? And why?'

'Like Dad, because it was the three of us. That's what they said, always just the three of us,' he said.

I felt his energy slipping a little as he repeated, 'Tell them I'm back, please. It's me, London.'

I thanked Taylor – or should I say London – for the communication and promised to pass his message on as instructed. I remember vividly calling Kevin and Marie to give them the results of the reading. It was all good news – and then I told them . . .

'Oh, one last thing. Taylor actually said his name is London and he has been with you before,' I said, wondering if I was right in what I was saying.

'Oh my . . .' Kevin stuttered.

'He said to tell you he's back. And his name, he said, is London, not Taylor,' I said again.

I could hear the phone being passed over to Marie.

'Joanne, it's Marie. What was that you said?' she asked.

And so I repeated what I had just told Kevin.

'London? London is back? It's really him? It is! I said it was, just last week. Everyone thought I'd lost my mind, but I was convinced. Just with things he would do. You know, certain mannerisms. He's identical!' she announced excitedly.

'So, let me ask you, was London an old dog of yours?'

'London was *the* dog. He was – is! – the dog my husband got me as an engagement present. A beautiful black Labrador. He even came to our wedding. Such a special day. Me, Kevin and London, just the three of us in our wedding pictures. So very special,' she explained.

'Can I ask if you dressed London up?' I asked, remembering what he had said about being dressed.

'Yes, well, he wore a matching bow tie the same cornflower blue as my husband's. He – well, they both looked so handsome!'

'Well, Marie, Taylor is in fact your dog London,' I explained. 'He is back.'

'Joanne, this is amazing. London has been dead for nearly eighteen years!' she said.

'Well, I'm simply the messenger, Marie, and according to Taylor, he is London.' And with that I left them to celebrate their news.

Two days later they called to thank me for the reading.

They said that Taylor was behaving just like London had done all those years before. Every little mannerism, every like and dislike was the same. In their minds there was absolutely no doubt that their dog had finally returned to them.

Over the years, whether it has been with dogs, cats, horses or other species, I have known animals to come back into the body of another animal. Sometimes this happens quite soon after death and at other times many years later. But Taylor was the one who first opened my eyes and heart to the reality of reincarnated dogs.

Whilst I know reincarnation does happen, in my experience it is much more common for the animals to appear in other animals, then disappear again just as quickly. So rather than coming back as the new dog, so to speak, the old animal simply shows itself through another.

I remember one example, from a family of four dogs who were all Lhasa apsos. This is a lovely breed of dog, small to medium-sized with a coat like Dougal from *The Magic Roundabout* (for those of you that remember that far back, like myself). The owners of the dogs had just lost one of the four to cancer and were finding it really hard to deal with.

One morning, whilst the lady owner was watching TV, she looked down at one of the three remaining dogs. Only what she saw was not the dog who was there, but the one that had died of cancer. As she explained it to me, it was as if the dog who had died had morphed into the live dog. The face, the coat, everything was him, and it was really clear. He looked up at her for a few seconds and then, as if by magic, he was gone. Afterwards, when she realised what had happened, she could still see her live dog sitting there, just as he had been before the apparition came.

For me, this is a regular occurrence. I get people emailing me nearly every week to tell me that they think it has happened to them and what should they do about it?

Well, I always say the same thing . . . Enjoy the experience! Your animal has come back to say he or she is OK. You have validation that they are indeed happy and well in the afterlife. So celebrate. It's a lovely gesture they have made to you.

One thing all these experiences have in common is that not one of them has happened a second time. It seems the animal comes back just the once and that's it. Why? Well, I think it is their way of letting you know they live on, maybe not on this earth, but somewhere else. And I truly think if you get this vision you should cherish it.

If animals don't come back, don't think it means they do not love you. They may not be able to get back, or it could be that they actually have come back and you just haven't noticed. For example, they may be sending you signs or symbols, like the ones you will read about later in this chapter, when my client was convinced her dog Ernie was sending her heart symbols. Or your dog may appear in your dreams, but you simply don't remember.

The passing of a dog can be one of the hardest things to come to terms with as a pet owner. These dogs find a way into our lives and into our hearts and they offer us unconditional love like no other. They may be with us for many years, sharing good times and bad, so when we lose them it can be devastating for all involved.

People often feel guilty about the decisions they have to make in their animal's last days. Please don't. I am often called out to animals that are terminally ill, just to double check whether they need help to pass. At some point you may find yourself in this sad situation, and I would urge you to use your own intuition and communication ability with your animal at this time.

In my experience, the animals will guide you to do what they want you to do. Your vet will also be able to help you make the right decision and do what is best. But you, and only you, know your dog. Ask him or her for the answers. Your dog will tell you the truth, because they always do. It is up to you as their carer to follow their wishes. Never allow others to make the decision for you – it's between you and your dog. For me this is simple . . . Just ask.

To help you a little with this, here is what I would advise you to do. Sit quietly with the animal and ask the questions below. After each question, listen carefully to the answer – and not only the answer you have in your heart but the one that pops into your mind. Be truthful with yourself.

- Are you ready to pass to spirit?
- Do you wish to have some help?
- Is there anything I can do for you?

Most of the time a dog's owners already have the answers in their hearts, but they want or need someone else to validate their feelings, almost giving them permission to let their dog pass.

Whenever you take your animal to the vet's surgery, for whatever reason, please make sure you tell them what you are doing. Explain where you are going and what will happen when you get there. This will make for a much more relaxed dog.

If an animal is near the end of their life, you may prefer to ask the vet out to your home. This is a very good option if your dog needs help to pass to spirit through euthanasia. Keep the room where he or she is quiet, play some soft music and allow your animal to pass with respect and dignity with those he or she loves.

I always ask my vet to give my animals a sedative before the final injection, to keep them calm and relaxed, but this is just the way I like to do it. This may be something you want to do, depending on the condition and situation of your dog at the time. Your vet will be able to advise you on this.

Sitting with your animal as he or she passes to spirit can be one of the most intimate and beautiful moments you will share together. Close your eyes and feel his energy as you say your goodbyes. When your animal passes you will notice a wonderful feeling of release. You will feel his energy leave and his soul disappear to another world. His body will become the shell that once held his beautiful soul. If you are connected through love, I promise you will see him on the other side, happy and well. Free from pain, injury or old age.

The two words respect and dignity are all you need to remember. Keep following your heart for the answers you are looking for at this difficult time and everything will be just fine.

In my experience, animals do not see death as we do. They live in the moment and when it is time to leave us, it is time. Death seems to be no big deal to them, as if they are just stepping out of one world and into another.

I occasionally come across animals who will hang on at the end of their life for the sake of their humans. It may be that their owner cannot let go and is not ready to live without their furry best friend just yet. For some owners, it's at this point that they might try what communicators know as 'bargaining'. It may be that a dog is dying and the human tries to bargain with the universe, with angels, with spirits or with god, saying things such as, 'Please, if you let my dog live, then I promise I will . . .' Many people go through the bargaining stage when their pet's death is imminent, in hope of a miracle. The animals will wait until their people are able to deal with the loss, but in the end they get the message across that it's time and the owners have to give in and let them pass.

I have to work on my own grief myself, with the answers I find through the animals and the support of friends. But thankfully I can help others who are grieving, by using communication and showing that the dogs do indeed live on in the spirit world. This is often a real comfort to those who are dealing with the loss of their dog.

I believe that some dogs stay close to us after their death, although this is not always the case. Perhaps they wish to help us through our grief. Then, once we feel a little better, they leave as they should do. For example, Hannah's dog Alfie, whose story is told earlier in this chapter, kept returning until she was able to deal with her loss and emotions and was ready to let him go for ever.

For some people, the death of a dog can be as hard to accept as the loss of a family member, and many people who lose their animals have no one to talk to about it either. Perhaps they live on their own and just can't bear to be without the companion they love so very much. This is all totally understandable. I still find it incredibly difficult to come to terms with the passing of a loved dog, even though I know how animals feel about death.

The grief of losing their beloved dog can sometimes hit people so hard that they cocoon themselves in their own home, not feeling able to move forward in life. With few friends and little support, they soon begin to feel depressed and emotionally drained.

This does not need to be the case at all. As fellow dog lovers, we all have a duty to help. It's sad, but so often I hear people say, 'It was just a dog! Pull yourself together.' But for the owner it's heartbreaking, because this wasn't 'just' a dog at all. This was their best – and sometimes their only – friend.

Some veterinary surgeries have a dedicated team of bereavement counsellors available for grieving clients. If they don't, they will probably be able to suggest someone who specialises in counselling people who have suffered the loss of an animal they loved dearly.

Grieving can be a complex process. The time it takes can vary, depending on each individual person and their emotional well-being and state of mind. When I used to work for Nestlé as a sales rep, I remember a colleague of mine lost her father to cancer on a Friday night. It was a great loss to her and all her family, yet to everyone's amazement she was able to return to work the following Monday. She was upset, obviously, but was able to continue doing her job, keeping herself busy. Just a few months later, my boss lost his mother and he was off work suffering with grief for three months. So, as you can see from this, no two people are the same, and every case needs to be looked at individually.

As someone who regularly deals with cases of pet loss, I

have found it is possible to see a pattern that consists of five main stages:

- Denial
- Guilt
- Anger
- Depression
- Closure

Some people will seem to be OK one minute, but then slip back to one of the earlier stages. This can happen over and over until closure is found.

A person who deals with the loss of their dog quickly may not have loved their dog any less than someone who cannot get over the dog's death. It's just a personal reaction, that's all. We each have our own ways of dealing with grief. Sometimes grieving lasts for only a few days, sometimes it may go on for a few months or, as I discovered recently, for years.

I think it's important to take a look at the process of grief so that we can at least understand what is going on, whether we experience it ourselves or we know someone else who is going through it.

Denial is a defensive mechanism our brains can use in an attempt to protect ourselves from the emotional trauma of losing a loved one, human or animal. We may convince ourselves that what has happened or is happening simply cannot be true, or that what we are hearing from our vet is wrong. Put simply, denial is a refusal to accept the truth.

Guilt is the most common feeling of all, in my experience. Having to make the awful decision to end a life is incomprehensible to most of us. No matter that it may be the best option, it will be the worst decision we have to take, and the feelings of guilt can overwhelm us so much that we can barely function in our day-to-day lives. We may find ourselves continually asking questions such as, Did I do the right thing? Was it the right time? What if I made a mistake? Did I make him suffer? and so forth.

Anger is one of the most common stages of grief. It can be directed at the vet, who may be blamed for not having done something to save the dog, at friends who offer advice, or at family members who are trying to help. Sometimes anger can be directed at ourselves as a form of guilt and in some cases the anger is with the dog itself, for dying.

Depression is not unusual when grieving our lost animals. For many of us, including myself, losing a pet is one of the saddest experiences we ever have to experience and depression can develop at any time and to varying degrees. We may feel a lack of interest in the outside world and find it difficult to concentrate, eat, sleep or carry out simple daily tasks. The help and understanding of other people is absolutely essential at this time, and yet we may want to remove ourselves from them. It has been medically proven that talking through your grief with someone else not only helps the healing process begin, but also enables you to move forward and accept what has happened.

Closure is the final and most significant stage of the pet grieving process. At this point, owners are able to accept that their beloved pet has died. We can finally begin to focus on the happy times we shared and enjoyed together, remembering how funny, cute and full of love our pets were. The owner may even consider looking for a new dog or puppy. This will never replace the dog that has passed, but it may fill an emotional space within us that the old dog has left behind. The anger, sadness or guilt may still occur but they are likely to pass more quickly than before. This is the time to look forward and renew that sense of unconditional love that our dogs give us. We all need to create a way to find closure, whether by planting a tree in memory of our pet, or perhaps having a painting done of the animal we've lost – some people like to scatter their animal's ashes in a place they both shared good times together, out on a favourite walk, on the beach or in the woods perhaps. Finding a way to remember the good times you shared together is paramount. However you choose to commemorate them, peace and remembrance will be sure to follow and life without your animal will become much easier to accept. Without closure, we are unable to fully draw a line under our stages of grief.

For even the most grief-stricken, communication can be valuable. Being able to contact a dog after death can help ease the pain tremendously. Communicating with your own dog that has passed is in most cases pretty easy. I would advise you to give yourself a few weeks, perhaps a few months, following the passing of your pet. You will be in a far better state of calmness to communicate and, as the key to communication is about being relaxed, waiting a little time before you try will help you create a better connection with your animal.

Here is how you could do it.

Have a good photograph of your dog to work with, and talk as you would when talking with a live animal. It may seem a little silly at first, but you might be surprised at what you hear and how comforting it can be.

It's really simple. Just ask the questions below and hear the answers. These may pop straight into your mind, or you may hear them through talking to yourself, as your own voice translates what your dog has to say.

It is often very useful to write your answers down, so it would be a good idea to have a notepad and pen to hand.

Give this exercise a go and experience the love you feel. And don't forget to thank your dog at the beginning of the exercise and again when you have come to the end.

- Thank you for sharing your life with me.
- What can you see where you are?
- Who are you with?
- Can you describe them?
- Is there anything I can do for you now you are in spirit?
- Have you any messages for me or other family members?
- I just want you to know how much I loved you.
- Thank you for communicating with me.

I do hope you have just experienced the same connection as I do. If so, I am sure you agree that it has to be the most amazing experience you can have with an animal that has passed to the spirit world.

Subtle encounters with poems, artwork or greeting cards can reflect an image of the animal we have lost. This seems to happen just when we need reassurance that our animal is OK. Are these coincidences? Or are we being sent messages or signs?

So many people tell me about their experiences of receiving signs shortly after their animals pass. For example, one lady was taking photographs of her children when she saw, in the background, a reflection of her little dog in the patio window. The dog had passed to spirit two weeks previously! Was it a sign that she was OK? I do feel the animals come back to give us a message that all is well and we can move on.

Here is an emotional true story that one of my clients, a lovely lady called Janette Rayton, wanted to share with me after her dog Ernie had passed. This is how it read:

Hi Joanne,

Just a quick email to let you know what happened with my dog Ernie. I did mention it briefly to you at the workshop you held when I met you, but I was a little too emotional then, and I know you understood that at the time. So here it is now. I'm ready to tell you.

As you know, Ernie, my dog, had been fighting kidney failure for a year and a half. We spent four days a week at the vet's and, bless him, he got so accepting of the tablets and injections, but he hated going there. He would grumble and was known as their favourite grumpy dog. Anyway, he unfortunately developed anaemia, then pancreatitis, but he still battled on and the vets said he wouldn't last much longer. They confirmed that they thought the time had now come to make the decision to have him euthanised.

I took him home that evening to think about it all and to my amazement he perked up. I didn't leave his side and he didn't leave mine for two weeks solid. I asked him to let me know when it was his time to go and he was so cuddly and loving that night. He could hardly walk, but I knew he wanted to take me somewhere. So later, when we were out in the garden, I let his lead go longer and he pottered over to my car. It was two o'clock in the morning and he looked at me, then the car, and I knew in my heart this was his way of telling me we had to get in and go to the vet's.

So without any reluctance I took him to the emergency vet and he didn't even grumble or fuss, which is something he would have normally done. When we arrived at the surgery he walked straight in, as if he was on a mission! This was so out of character. He never walked in like this before. I knew in my heart he was ready to pass and needed the vet's help to do so.

I wrapped him in his blanket and gave him a kiss and a cuddle, telling him just how brave he was and how much I loved and adored him. Ernie was quietly and calmly euthanised and I requested that he was cremated. His ashes were put in a beautiful wooden casket with the words 'Ernie, my angel, you live on in the hearts you leave behind' engraved on it.

I went to work the next day to keep busy but I felt his loss ever so much. That day, I looked up to the sky and there, straight above me, was a cloud in exactly the shape of Ernie when he was young. I couldn't help thinking how odd but amazing this was as I stared at it. Luckily it remained long enough for me to take a picture with my camera phone, but seconds later it dispersed into the other clouds in the sky and was gone.

Every Wednesday since 30 June when Ernie passed over, I am sure I have received a heart or three hearts with the number three on them. These appear mainly from petals that drop from my flowers in the house in the shapes of hearts or stones on the beach.

When we went to our local Chinese restaurant, our table was the only one with hearts above it as decoration and a heart candleholder on the table. All the others had birds on them. Was it a sign? Later that night, when we arrived home, I found a heart trinket with a West Highland terrier just like Ernie on it in my cupboard, and inside was a pack of playing cards with three hearts and a heart gift bag, which had a picture on it of a little dog wearing heart glasses!

A week later, we went on a walk and noticed a leaf,

which had been pinned on a telegraph pole. It was in the shape of a heart, and the road sign above had a heart sticker on. The following week, the chair I sat in at the bingo hall I attend had a carved-out heart on it. The hotel room we stayed at shortly after had a showerhead with engraved hearts and that night the moon above my head was in a perfect heart shape.

These odd occurrences just keep happening all the time. They come out of nowhere. Even today, a cheese string, for instance, took the shape of a perfect heart! This may well be coincidence, but wow, I feel Ernie may just have taken the words on his casket 'You live on in the hearts you leave behind' literally! Whatever it is, it makes me feel wonderful.

Now whether all this was a sign from Ernie himself or not, one thing's certain – it sure gave his mum comfort.

This is sometimes a very lonely time. People do not always understand your loss, and only you had the special connection with the animal. Please remember you are never alone. Call in your friends or family members to walk the road of grief with you. Remember that it's OK to cry, it's OK to have days of sadness, it's OK to love.

Here are a few ways to comfort yourself after you have lost an animal:

- **Bach Flower Remedies** are a great support for mental/emotional/physical/spiritual balance. They will help restore peace, balance, clarity, courage and strength, for you and your animals. Available from most chemists. But seek veterinary advice in the first instance and they will be able to advise you on a suitable natural treatment.
- **Surround yourself with healing colours** that will give you warmth and peace.
- **Play your favourite music** to relax and energise you.
- **Plant a tree or shrub** in memory of your animal and watch it grow. This will make a nice place to go and sit when you need a little 'me' time.
- **Write a story** about the life of the animal. All the fond memories will come flooding back, and it's a great way to heal your heart.
- **Share your feelings** with others who have lost animals.
- **Start a forum** about losing pets on the Internet.
- **Build a website** in memory of your pet, including stories and photographs. You will be amazed at the support you find.

- **Make a book** dedicated to the dog's memory, containing all the photos you have of him or her.
- **Talk** to an animal bereavement counsellor, friend or relative.

We hold the essence of our dogs in our hearts through the memories of their furry faces, sparkly eyes and wet noses. Their trust, loyalty and sharing of love and pain are the most precious memories we can hold on to.

No one said you had to throw away the unused bed, the empty bowl or the lead hanging on the hook. If you want to keep them, do. For months after his death, I still had Mr Klein's bed sitting in my living room. Without it, I felt alone. It stayed there until I found my own closure and not before. So do what comforts you, not what others want you to do. This is your grief, not theirs. Please know you are never alone.

It is unfortunately true that some dogs suffer grief for a lost one, just as we do. I know it was nearly two weeks before my dog Mozart could eat properly or play happily after the loss of his kennel mate, Mosko. Sometimes the grief can be so severe that the dog is desperately ill.

I received a phone call from a client in a terrible situation. Her dog Ben had sadly passed over to spirit earlier that month, and her other dog, Simba, was suffering badly. Both dogs were Great Danes and had been together since they were just fourteen weeks old. The five happy years they spent together were full of endless fun. They were inseparable, and truly had a lovely connection as best friends and companions. However, out of the blue, Ben suffered a major heart attack which took his life, leaving poor Simba standing over him, grief-stricken at his best friend's death. There was nothing that could have been done to save Ben that day, and he was buried on the owner's farm, under the willow tree by the pond that he and Simba used to play around.

Simba fell instantly into a deep depression, not wishing to eat, drink much, play or interact with humans or even dogs. No matter what the family tried, no amount of love and TLC would bring him round. He was full of grief.

Within a week his health was failing. The vet couldn't find anything wrong and put it down to the emotional trauma of losing his companion. Two weeks went by and he had dropped so much of his body weight that he hardly had enough energy to stand. Three weeks in, with no sign of improvement, they called me.

The first thing I wanted to do for Simba was to tell him it was OK to grieve. This is so important. So many people try and snap dogs out of it, just as we try to do with humans, but sometimes we need to allow the grief to show through before the healing process can begin.

I told him I understood his pain and loss and that Ben would be OK in spirit. I also said that Ben wouldn't wish his friend to be ill, so I asked Simba to have a good meal and consider helping his mum over Ben's death. I said she needed his help now. I knew that by doing this he would not be dwelling on his own loss, but on that of his human mum, therefore diverting himself without realising it. That, in turn, would help him to come to terms with the loss of his best friend.

That evening, Simba went up to his owner, laid his head on her lap and gave a huge sigh. She broke down in tears as she cuddled and comforted Simba. The next day, after a good breakfast, both were able to walk down to the pond where Ben had been buried and spend time remembering him. Within days Simba was regaining his strength and had a healthy appetite again. He and his owner faced the loss of Ben together but life went on and in the end closure was found for both.

So sometimes a little help directing the grief in the right direction is all it takes. It certainly worked for Simba and his mum.

You must always allow your dog to grieve if necessary.

Reassure them they are loved and always will be loved. Take the time to be with them. Like people, dogs often feel lonely and miss the physical presence of their furry friend.

Your vet may also have some suggestions, and Bach Flower Remedies can help a lot.

Chapter Seven

In my workshops and when being consulted by clients I see many dogs with problems which are quite straightforward. They may be misbehaving on the lead, having trouble sleeping or just be frightened. This is all quite normal in the life of a communicator such as myself. Whatever the dog's problem, it can almost always be dealt with through communication techniques.

I often work with dogs who have the same behaviour problems as our old dog Sally. Back then, all those years ago, the only animal trainer I remember seeing on TV was the famous Barbara Woodhouse. She was probably one of the first celebrity dog trainers of our time and scared the living daylights out of most people, let alone the dogs!

For those of you too young to remember Barbara Woodhouse, imagine a larger-built lady, very strict schoolmistress type, dressed in a smart tweed skirt and waistcoat, with a voice that you would not want to disobey in any way. I'm quite sure she was lovely in person, but boy, you would do as you were told! Anyway, her dog training techniques were known throughout the land and she was a regular on TV and in magazines. Her methods of tough training, using choker chains and yanking the dogs into submission with sharp commands of 'sit' or 'stay', certainly produced results.

Thankfully times have moved on and the old methods of training have changed with them. Today we use ways of teaching and imprinting dogs which enhance their lives and those of their owners too. Dogs are capable of becoming fabulous members of our society, and they always amaze me with their ability to genuinely transform from so-called untrainable dogs to well-behaved friendly family dogs in a short space of time. They love structure, guidelines and clear instruction.

Within the horse world people use the phrase 'Love, language and leadership' when talking about training animals. However much love you show your animal, it won't have the skill to become a balanced, well-mannered animal unless you also give it clear instructions about how to behave and show it some leadership. In a dog's case, the pack leader is the human.

Animal Communication, which is what I teach and do, is an excellent way of combining training methods with communication skills to produce brilliant results.

My daily work as a professional Animal Communicator is always varied, but I thought I would list the most common problems I come across, with the solutions I suggest. There are also some case histories, showing how I deal with these problems using my expertise and knowledge of communication.

I hope this may help you with your dog if you are currently experiencing the same issues. But whenever you have a problem with your dog, please remember that it is essential to seek veterinary help in the first instance. If your vet agrees, work such as mine can be introduced to enhance what the vet offers.

Top Ten Problems
1. Separation anxiety
2. Vet or kennel panic
3. Choosing a new dog for the family
4. Soiling the house
5. Pulling on the lead and general obedience
6. Car sickness
7. Name change
8. Rescue dog introduction
9. Depression
10. Rehoming your dog

Separation anxiety This takes the number-one spot of all my requests for help and it can be really difficult to get under control. But with patience and practice it can be overcome.

Firstly, let's understand what separation anxiety is. This is a condition in which your dog gets very worked up when left on his own. He may rip up carpets, chew items in the house, dig at doors and windows in order to escape, panic, whimper or howl in the hope his owner will come home. He may pant uncontrollably or even soil numerous times, unable to control himself and his emotions.

Unfortunately, this is pretty common and needs addressing as soon as possible. One thing we must be clear about is that your dog is not doing any of these things to get at you for leaving him alone. No, he is behaving like this because he is terrified of being left on his own, with no idea if you will ever come back. In other words, he is scared.

This is how I help to solve the problem, using communication techniques and traditional holistic methods. Each will enhance the other.

First and foremost, you need to establish who is pack leader in your home. This may seem an odd thing to say, but let's look at this for a moment. In the wild, dogs have a clear pack order in the family. The leaders come first, then the younger dogs, and so on. Right at the bottom of the pack are the pups. The leaders take control and are quite able to make decisions or leave the pack, as and when they choose, whereas the followers do not have that choice. It is their job to follow and to stay within the pack.

If a leader loses his following pack, he will become panicky and stressed, just as your dog does with separation anxiety. This normally happens because your dog has stepped into the role of pack leader within the home and family, and this is something you have allowed him to do.

As pack leader, his behaviour usually consists of being very overexcited about seeing you – greeting you when you come home with the world's best hellos, jumping all over you, sometimes squealing in excitement, even peeing. Now, whilst I am quite sure you think this is flattering and tells you your dog loves you (which we know he does), it isn't a good thing. I bet you return his amazing greeting in just the same way, giving him kisses and cuddles and lavishing him with love and affection when you have hardly got through the door.

Trust me, this does not help! This will only prove to him that this is the best time of his day and the rest of the day will be spent in deep depression and anxiety.

So we need to get some balance back, and quickly.

Start off by re-establishing the pack order. The only leaders in the home should be the humans. Simple. Dogs work with communication and with natural instinct too. When you or your family are in the home with your dog, have some rules.

This brings in the idea of offering love, language and leadership, which I mentioned a little earlier. Many horse people use this naturally, and it works perfectly for dogs, too.

Firstly, don't let your dog follow you everywhere, watching your every move. For instance, you'd be surprised how a simple thing like letting him into the washroom when you go to the loo can affect the balance of the relationship. Shut the door and leave him outside! Let him wait for you. You are the leader, you are in control.

When you prepare his dinner, think about this for a second . . . In a wild pack, who eats first, the leaders or the followers? Exactly! The leaders. So always have something to eat before you put his dinner down, and make sure he sees you clearly, even if it's as simple as a biscuit from the cupboard. Then let him eat when you are ready, not when he says so.

When you give him attention, do so when he is calm. If you give a dog love when he is behaving like a loony, you are only reinforcing bad behaviour. So allow him to relax, then give him all the cuddles and kisses you wish.

And the main thing is to stop giving him the instant crazy greeting when you return home. Go into the house in a low-key, quiet way. Totally ignore his behaviour and try hard not to look him in the eye. Be quiet and simply go about your business for two or three minutes or until he calms down. Then, when he is calm, go cuddle! By doing this you are reinforcing calmness, so that it's pleasant when you arrive home, instead of being chaotic. Very quickly he will click that if he behaves quietly he gets his cuddle.

Use your communication as you leave the house in the morning. When your dog is calm, send him a thought that you will be back at a certain time, so that he knows when you are coming home. This will reinforce you as the pack leader as well as letting him know you are not deserting him totally.

Remember to follow your leadership rules whenever you leave your dog. Go without a fuss, don't draw attention to the fact you are leaving, use communication at this point and slip away quietly.

Within a few days you will start to see a real improvement. After a few weeks your dog will be able to cope so much more easily when you leave him for various periods. It's always good to start off at weekends and practise leaving him for short periods of time, allowing him to become accustomed to the rules.

I also recommend that you always tell your animals where you are going and when you are coming back. It really makes a difference, whether your pet suffers from separation anxiety or is anxious about a trip to the vet or kennels. Explain what is going to happen, for how long and why, and you will soon see a difference in your dog.

Dogs are social animals who need lots of interaction with their owners to be happy, so if you know your dog will be alone for long periods whilst you are at work, it would be a great idea to have somebody come in to walk him during the day, breaking up the time and relieving his boredom or loneliness. Or perhaps you could take him to a local doggy day care; such places are becoming more and more popular.

Given his name, you will not be surprised that Collie was a lovely black and white border collie. Unfortunately, he had a real anxiety about his owner leaving him. He would shake, hide himself away from whoever was looking after him and refuse to eat until his owner's return. This was stressful for the dog and also for his owner, who felt guilty about having to leave him for work.

I connected to Collie, using communication, to find out why he felt like this, and it was simply because he thought his owner was never going to come home. So I asked her to send thoughts to Collie, using simple visualisation.

'Send him a thought of you leaving, and show him in your mind's eye how many sleeps you will be away for,' I suggested, explaining to her that each sleep meant a night in Collie's mind. 'Then finish with a lovely picture of you returning, happy and pleased to see him.'

I also asked her to visualise him eating whilst she was away, interacting with his carer and being calm, and told her not to make a big deal out of her forthcoming trip. This would make her and the dog more relaxed.

A few days before she was due to go on her next trip, she repeated all the visualisations several times. When the departure day came, she noticed a real change in Collie's behaviour. Instead of shaking and looking frantic that she was going, he just stood and wagged his tail. She left, bemused but hopeful that the techniques had indeed helped.

I had requested that she also thought about Collie whilst she was away, visualising him being relaxed and calm, eating well and in all-round general good health.

Three days passed and on the owner's return Collie was like a different dog. The carer said he had been absolutely fine. He had seemed relaxed and even stayed by her side most of the time, something he never used to do. Collie was so much more happy and content, which in turn helped his owner focus on her work and not worry too much about leaving him.

Vet or kennel panic This condition will only get worse if it is not dealt with. Your dog will become more and more stressed about trips to the vet or the kennels, making himself quite anxious and even ill. This can really pose a problem for owners, who may not be able to take their loved dog for routine check-ups or vaccinations. More importantly, if something awful happened it would create all types of worry for both owner and dog.

Firstly, going to the vet's or the kennels is no big deal, and this is what you have to get through to your dog. He has to trust you and trust your decisions. No matter what happens, he will be safe. If he's going to the vet's, he needs to trust you to take care of him. If it's the kennels, he needs to know you will be back for him.

The golden rule is to start as we did with separation anxiety and behave like the pack leader. Follow the rules and create a leadership he can follow. He will then be able to trust your judgement in different situations and let go of his anxiety and feeling of responsibility.

Use communication to reinforce your leadership

judgement. For instance, if you are taking him on a trip to the vet's, send him a thought in your mind of the journey to the vet's. Follow the whole scenario in your mind's eye, making it calm and positive, and show him what will happen when he gets there. Half the time, when dogs go into panic mode, it's simply because they are afraid of the unknown. Finish with him coming home and getting praise for being good. Run this through your mind, sending it to him many times over. He will get the visualisation and begin to calm down.

If he is going to the kennels, do the same exercise but this time tell him when you will be coming home. I like to say this in sleeps. So, for instance, 'I will be home in five sleeps' tells the dog that you will be back for him after five nights. That way your dog will know he has not been abandoned. You can also tell him that he must eat well, stay healthy and enjoy his holiday. All the positive encouragement makes for a stress-free dog.

Bobby is a small five-year-old King Charles spaniel who was terrified of going to the vet's. Like Collie, who suffered from separation anxiety, this was simply because he didn't understand what was happening. So the same rules apply here as they did for Collie in the previous case history.

I asked Bobby's owners to visualise the whole visit to the vet, starting with seeing Bobby sitting happily inside the car on the way there. Then they were to visualise him arriving at the surgery, meeting and greeting the vet nurses, being taken into the consulting room and having whatever treatment he needed. All the while, they were seeing him happy, relaxed and calm. This exercise was repeated over and over. To top it all, they explained to him that he would only be there for a short time and that they would not leave him.

His improvement was brilliant. Within days he was much happier, calmer and more willing to go to the vet for his routine treatment.

Choosing a new dog for the family Looking for a new dog can be one of the most difficult challenges a family will face. Getting the breed, temperament and match right is not easy for some people. But using communication and a little common sense can really help. It is so important that the dog you choose matches the family in ways such as size and breed, but personality is also very important.

Now I like to think of this as being like the TV show *Big Brother*. The producers place a bunch of complete strangers in a house and wait to see if they get on. Some do, of course, and they go on to form lasting friendships, but others instantly take a dislike to one another. They may be so unhappy about being in the house that they break out or end up in a total mess, crying and close to a breakdown.

Choosing a dog for the family in the wrong way is no different, really. Most people decide on a breed and then buy the first dog they see. The dog moves in and wham! there is an instant personality clash. This ends with the dog being absolutely miserable and all sorts of trouble develops because the owners can't connect with the dog. I have known people to speak really badly about their dog, through no fault of its own, and I have known dogs to keep running away, trying everything they can to get away from their family. So a little thought and care is needed when choosing.

Do all your research first. Find out all about the breed and its characteristics. Consider whether that particular breed will fit into your lifestyle. Factors like the length of your working day, the presence of children and whether you live in a quiet or busy house all need to be taken into account. Speak with the breeders, making sure you get all your questions answered. If they are open and honest with you, then this is a good sign.

Once the breed has been sourced and you really feel it is the right one for you, then communication comes in. Go and see the parents with the puppies, and simply ask the puppies which one of them wishes to come and live with you. It's that simple. The right one will walk straight up to you and let you know. You will instantly feel a connection in your heart. Go with your gut feeling – it's always the right decision.

Doing it this way, your pup will be choosing you. So don't get blinded because he may not be the colour you were thinking about or the biggest puppy in the litter. Just ask, and the right matching pup will soon be in your arms!

A lovely family came to ask for my help a few years ago. They had been to see two puppies but could not make up their minds which one to choose.

The first puppy was short-legged, long-bodied and of mixed breeding, a little like a dachshund. He had a lovely sweet expression and a kind face. The children were instantly in love with him and, being a typical puppy, he adored all the attention they gave him.

But, as I sat to one side, I noticed that the parents weren't interacting with the puppy. Yes, they thought he was cute, but I thought they weren't really bothered with him.

'What do you feel about him?' I asked.

'Well, to be honest, not much really. He's nice and the

children seem to love him, but I am just not sure,' the dad replied.

'OK. What about you?' I said, looking at the mum.

'Yes, I like him. He makes the children happy,' she said.

I had the feeling that the parents were both looking at the dog through the eyes of the children and so were not actually choosing the dog that fitted the whole family. Instead they were choosing on puppy appeal. Trust me when I say this is not the way to do it.

There was nothing coming from the heart of either of them, so we went over to the home of the second puppy. He was a gorgeous Labrador type, and obviously a lot larger. He was kind, just like the other one had been, with a sweet, happy personality and full of fun. What I noticed straightaway was a role reversal. The father was immediately drawn in, scratching the dog's floppy ears and calling him Bud. This was a match made in heaven. The parents of the children were happily playing with the puppy. The children, on the other hand, who were both under ten years old, sat and watched as this puppy piled all his affection on the adults.

'So, how do you two feel about this little feller, then?' I asked the parents.

Instantly the pair replied, 'He's wonderful, Joanne.'

'So where's your problem?' I smiled.

They both looked over at the children, who were sitting chatting about other things. 'They want the other puppy, so we just don't know what to do,' they replied.

So I sent a visualisation picture of the two girls through to the puppy, to see its reaction. At first, nothing happened. Then, all of a sudden, the puppy rushed over and dived on top of one of the girls. She fell backwards from her sitting position, laughing at the face-washing she was receiving, while her sister began laughing uncontrollably too at the funny sight.

'There – I think you have your answer. Your gut feeling was for this puppy, right? Well, you must always go with your gut instinct.'

I felt this was definitely the better puppy for them. He interacted with everyone and he was taller. So, looking at the family and their activity level, he would be able to join in more. And best of all, the puppy adored all four family members.

Bud, as he was to be named, joined the family as its fifth member, and he fitted into the group perfectly.

Soiling the house This is a common problem and one that I deal with so often. It's pretty simple to sort out if you are consistent with your actions and your communication.

Dogs and puppies can find it hard to understand what is expected of them. Some will soil your home through laziness, and some through fear. Some may have medical problems and others are just simply not able to hold out for the time that you want them to. (In the latter case, the problem is your responsibility and should be addressed as soon as possible.)

Your dog or puppy needs to have regular toilet breaks throughout the day and night, depending on age and condition. Let him out for a toilet break after every sleep or feed. This works especially well for puppies, as some will really struggle to hold out for long. This is also a good idea with older dogs. Create a routine for your dog.

Remember to give your dog praise. Now, you may think it silly to be talking in a funny high-pitched voice to your dog for doing his business, but let me assure you, if your dog thinks he is pleasing you, he will be looking forward to going out the next time. After a while, he will know this is what you absolutely love him to do.

Puppy pads, which are available through good pet shops and online, are a type of large square absorbent disposable mat. These are good for very young pups. Place them by the door where they will be going out, to help catch any mistakes that young pups are likely to have.

Never rub their noses in mistakes. It will only make the dog or puppy fear you. He won't understand what you are doing, and it is the worst type of behaviour from humans. If you were potty training your two-year-old child and he had a little accident, can you imagine rubbing his face in it? No, so why on earth would you do this to a puppy? Puppies may be different in the physical sense but they think, feel and hurt just as humans. Praise the positive behaviour, making no big deal out of mistakes, and your dog will quickly realise what you desire.

Always send a clear vision to your dog of what you need it to do. For instance, visualising your dog doing its business outside, over and over, will create an understanding.

One thing I hear a lot from clients is, 'Our last dog used to wait for six hours before needing to go out, but this one just does it all the time.' Well, like humans, all dogs are different. Just because one can hold out for hours, it does not mean another can. You have to work out what suits your particular dog best.

I think pups and dogs should not be left without toilet breaks for more than a few hours. If the soiling is happening when you are out at work, then you need to find someone to let your dog out for regular breaks, until he is able to hold himself a little longer each time.

Now, if you have an older dog with this problem, please get a vet to check him over to see that there are no medical conditions causing him to relieve himself often. Once this has been ruled out, start from scratch as you would with a puppy. Let him out after every sleep and meal, and remember to praise him (and reward him if necessary) until he feels confident. If you are out at work, then doggy day care or someone coming to let him out regularly will make such a difference.

I always like to have my clients use communication to connect with their dogs, visualising what they desire from them. You can even ask the older dog why he is soiling the house, and he may give you a reason that you are then able to correct. Visualisation allows the dog to understand what you expect from him, so that he doesn't feel he is constantly disappointing you without actually realising why!

So, training your dog to go outside should not become a battle of wills. It is about developing a positive understanding of what is expected and acceptable. Love and positive actions always work well.

Two cases come to mind when I think about dogs who have had a problem with toilet training. The first one, called Hamish, was a small, white West Highland terrier. His owners were always in a rush and quite forgetful about time, so it came as no surprise that Hamish was swept up in their whirlwind of a home.

When I asked Hamish why he soiled the house, he answered, 'Well, where else can I do it?'

My reply was that outside, on the owners' designated lawn area, would be the best solution.

He looked me straight in the eye and said, 'And how do you propose I get out there, then?'

After talking to his owners, we soon realised that Hamish had not been given any regular toilet breaks. When his owners remembered, they would open the door and let him out. However, because they were so busy, they would call him back in as soon as possible, not having given him time to do anything. Hence the accidents in the house.

This case was simple to remedy. I used visualisation to show Hamish that he needed to go on the lawn, and gave the owners a timetable of when to let him out to do his business. And luckily for Hamish the owners stuck to it, feeling a little embarrassed that the problem was indeed with them and not Hamish.

The second dog was Munchkin, a tiny Yorkie who hated the rain and would pee on the carpet rather than go outside. No amount of coaxing worked. She just refused, point blank, to get wet.

This case was equally simple. I told the owners that, rather than asking Munchkin to go out in the rain whilst standing at the door, they needed to put their coats on and join her until she had been to the loo. To my mind, this is only fair. In other words, if you won't go outside in the rain yourself, why do you expect your dog to?

There is no doubt that Munchkin hates the rain and, to be honest, this is something that will probably never change. However, the fact that the owners were willing to be there with her made such a difference. I instructed them to wait until she had actually done her business before returning to the house. The longer she refused, the longer she waited in the rain. As you can imagine, it soon triggered her intelligent mind to go quickly, as the quicker it was done the sooner she was able to get back into the house.

With both these simple cases, visualisation and some good old-fashioned praise was used to reinforce what we were asking the dogs to do.

Pulling on the lead and general obedience I always use general communication when working with a dog. I absolutely hate saying the word obedience! I much prefer to think my dogs are working with me as a team rather than being obedient. Co-operation is much better.

I never use training aids such as check (choke) chains or anything harsh. A well-designed body harness that secures the dog neatly around the chest area or a new-style head collar that prevents the dog's neck bending when you hold its lead is best — ask your local pet shop or vet for examples and advice. Both of these, provided they are fitted correctly, can work well for really strong dogs. But letting your dog understand exactly what you expect from him is the most important bit. The three steps I like to use are:

- Visualisation
- Positive reinforcement
- Reward and praise

First, I send a positive picture thought through to my dog using visualisation, so that the dog is able to see what I am asking for. Perhaps it will be the thought of him walking nice and calmly by my side, with a loose lead, so that we are happy to walk along together. I keep sending this thought over and over before we go out.

During the walk I offer a lovely reward, such as a little cheese, every time he corrects himself into walking by my side. When he does this I praise him as well. This helps him to understand that he is doing exactly what I am asking him to do. And all the while I am sending the visualisation of what is expected. You'll be amazed how quickly dogs pick it up.

Never yank the dog back on the lead. You can really do injury to the dog's neck and spine by doing this. Take the time to show your dog in a positive way what you would like and you will never have to experience the undesired pulling behaviour.

Zara, a large, very good-looking Rottweiler was a really strong lead puller. In fact, she was so strong that she had pulled her owner over on numerous occasions.

Zara was a good dog in all other respects, and you could say she was just being a bit too enthusiastic. She certainly wasn't being bad or misbehaving. She just didn't understand what was expected from her.

I asked the owners to follow my guidelines, given above, over a period of a week, spending ten minutes each day visualising her walking quietly by their side. Every time Zara moved closer to their leg, trying to do what they were sending her through thought, they rewarded her with lots of praise and a lovely piece of cheese.

It quickly became apparent that, being a smart dog,

she had worked out for herself that it was much nicer to be at her owner's side than pulling out in front. And soon Zara was walking perfectly. The cheese rewards became less frequent, which in turn made her even more determined to walk perfectly, in the hope that at any moment the lovely waft of Cheddar might come from her owner's hand without warning and delight her taste buds one last time. But, most of all, through visualisation she could understand what was expected of her. It's simple to do and effective.

Car sickness Just like some people, dogs can suffer car sickness. Now, this can be a simple case of motion sickness, or it may be the result of a bad experience, such as being left alone in the car for too long or when it is too hot.

(On that point, never ever leave dogs in a car on hot days. They can be dead in less than ten minutes! And remember that a temperature that is just warm to us could be overwhelming for some dogs. So please, just don't do it! Leave them at home or take them out of the car with you.)

Car sickness is something that communicators often deal with. I suggest you first try to understand why your dog doesn't like going in the car, by simply asking the question using communication. Car sickness can be caused simply by the motion, but it can also be caused by fear. Some dogs have experienced their owner's bad driving, for example; it's easy to forget that dogs have to balance in the car a little to be comfortable. Most dogs will lie down, but some puppies and dogs prefer to stand or sit, and so if you are whizzing around corners your dog is constantly having to correct himself, which can sometimes be so traumatic that it stimulates car sickness and a fear of travel. By knowing what the cause is, you will be able to help ease the problem if not cure it completely. Always drive with care and consideration for your dog when he is travelling with you.

Once you have established the cause, visualise your dog going into the car, staying calm and relaxed, and then coming back out. Keep sending these thoughts whilst actively practising putting him in the car but not actually taking him anywhere just yet. Place him in the car for a few minutes, keeping all the doors open, so he gets used to being in the car.

Make sure that there is a good base for him to stand, sit or lie on, such as a dog pad or quilt. I like to buy a budget single quilt from the supermarket. This gives a nice soft base and can be popped into the washing machine when it gets dirty.

Work your way up to around five minutes in the car, giving your dog plenty of reward and praise. Then start doing it all over again, but this time with the car doors closed. Repeat with the engine on, until eventually you take the dog for a short drive of just a few minutes. The length of time the whole process takes will depend on the dog.

The most important thing is to keep visualising him being calm and relaxed. If you stress about it, he will pick up that image and feeling and you will be straight back at square one! Be consistent and encourage the relaxed behaviour, and before long your dog will be calm enough to travel.

Take your dogs to fun places, rather than only going in the car to the vet's. That way he will look forward to his day out, rather than associating the car with trips to the surgery. You can continue the positive thought process by sending images of where you are going to take him, such as the beach or fields.

Cassie, one of the rescue lurchers I described earlier, suffered from car sickness. Her body went into complete shakes whenever she even saw the car. So, just like other dogs I have worked with, we began the process of teaching her that being in a car was OK. It was nothing scary and something she would be able to deal with.

I spent days sending positive thoughts to her through communication. I sent many thoughts of her sitting in the car, lying in the car and sleeping in the car, at the same time telling her she was calm, relaxed and happy.

Then when I went to visit her, I would sit her in the car on a rug for about five minutes, but not go anywhere. I repeated this over and over until she could eventually sit in the car with the engine running.

Her shaking began to ease and within a few days we were able to take her for short drives around the block. We extended the drives just a little each day. As soon as she could cope with this, we began to take her to nice places.

It really is that simple. Now Cassie can travel without being sick or being stressed about the journey. It just takes consistency on your part.

Name change Many of you will be surprised to see this among my top ten problems, but it is something I come across so very often.

In my experience, many rescue dogs want to change their names when they arrive at a new family. Now, it's not always the case, but it is very common. This is because they wish to start afresh, looking forward and not back.

Or perhaps your dog's name just doesn't suit him. It's not bad luck to change a pet's name. It's doing something that is right for the pet.

No matter what the reason, I find that most dogs will tell you what they wish to be called if you ask. Yes, it seems odd, but it really is as simple as that. Say something like, 'What is your name?' and see what they say back to you.

You may be surprised that whilst your new dog is called Bob, for example, he sees himself as Baby, because that was what his owners called him way back as a pup. In cases like this you have your answer.

Or the dog may say he hates his name and wants a new one. If this is the case, you can negotiate a suitable name. He will soon tell you if he likes what you come up with. Dogs are more than capable of giving you the answer. Again, go with your gut feeling on this one.

I had the delight of meeting Teeth (yes, that's what I said – a dog called Teeth!) because his owners were having problems with him. Whenever anyone came to the house he would warn them off by showing his teeth. So, when I found out that the dog's name was Teeth, I knew instantly that the name had to be changed. In my experience, names do sometimes affect a dog's behaviour.

Think about this for a moment . . . How many animals can you think of with really cute names? Isn't it true that in most cases they themselves are cute and nice? Now think about those animals with rough, hard names, and you will see their names reflect their personality too. I'm not saying this is true for every dog, but a name is often a key to the overall energy of the dog. (You can do this exercise with people, too, which can be quite funny.)

Anyway, Teeth by name, Teeth by nature. So it was agreed we would change his name.

If possible, I ask the animals to choose a name they like. But in this case Teeth was not bothered. The owners agreed it should sound similar to Teeth but be something that suited him and the way they wished him to be – funny, relaxed and happy-go-lucky.

Teeth had a longish strawberry blonde coat, which was a little windswept, you could say, and a funny personality (except when he was showing his teeth). We all laughed when we realised he actually looked rather like a certain comedy character whose name rhymes with Teeth. Yes, he looked like Keith Lemon, one of the characters in *Bo' Selecta!* It was perfect. And so he became Keith the dog.

Within days his personality began to mellow and he became a calm, funny dog, who enjoyed greeting people at the door. He liked his new name.

Rescue dog introduction This comes back to choosing the right dog for your family, especially if you have other dogs. Your new dog may fit your personality, but that does not mean to say he will fit in with your dog at home. Be very careful. You need to look at what your own dog is like and choose a rescue dog that complements your dog's nature.

The rescue centre will help you with this and can advise which dogs could be suitable. For instance, some dogs are terrified of certain other breeds. And there would be no point in putting two dominant dogs together. So please, take your time and follow your instinct.

When matching dogs, I like to visualise the dogs, sending them clear images of the two of them getting along happily, playing together and becoming good friends. By sending through thoughts of what you want, both dogs will understand what is expected from them.

A good match can be a wonderful thing to see. In my opinion, all dogs should have a doggy friend. Not a human, but a fellow dog. A dog that has previously been lonely may find a whole new lease of life with his new buddy!

Many of us fear having two dogs, but trust me when I say it's much easier. They play together and keep each other company. Having a doggy companion can also help a dog with separation anxiety. He no longer misses his owners quite so much as he is not on his own. And above all, dogs speak the same language. No matter how much we are able to communicate and understand them, there is nothing like one of their own.

Just reverse the thought and put yourself in your dog's shoes. Imagine never having another human for company in a house of dogs, for eighteen years or so. Ohh, the thought! So why do we do it with dogs? This is a personal decision, of course, but one that is worth thinking about.

And best of all, you will all have so much fun!

A few years ago I had the great pleasure of meeting a rescue dog called Boogie. It would be an understatement to say that Boogie had a reputation. He was a medium-sized brown dog of stocky build, with a head that looked like it was made from steel and a temperament like Arnold Schwarzenegger in *The Terminator* when he said that classic line, 'I'll be back'.

And sure enough Boogie always was. The rescue centre who had cared for him since he was found as a stray had tried to rehome this dog over and over again, but they were always unsuccessful. Each time, he was brought back due to his unpredictable behaviour. He had two counts to his name of attacking dogs he had been rehomed with, one count of escape and another of chewing half a sofa to shreds.

I was called in as a last resort, because the next option was to have him put to sleep. In my opinion, Boogie certainly wasn't a bad dog. He just had not been matched with the right family. He needed a family that suited his character, one that was a little like him, you could say. Whilst the rescue centre thought they were doing the right thing by letting him go to nice, calm, quiet homes, for this particular dog it would be like sending the Jedward twins to live with Margaret Thatcher or the late Princess Diana. They just wouldn't fit together.

After spending some time with Boogie and really getting to know his personality, I was able to describe the type of people he should be rehomed with. It took several months, and then the perfect pair came walking through the centre's doors. They were a couple of heavy rockers. Both the man and woman were dressed head to toe in leather and they would probably look a little scary to some people, but they had hearts of gold. They already had a dog, a female pitbull type, and wanted a companion for her. Boogie was the perfect dog!

I offered to talk to the new potential owners and explained Boogie's personality. I told them he was dominant, headstrong and fearless, that he had a liking for the ladies and, most importantly, adored chicken chow mein! (Yes, I know the last bit about the chow mein was a bit unusual, but hey, I was just passing on the information Boogie had given me when speaking with him.) The couple seemed perfect for him and so Boogie was adopted. I also explained to Boogie where he would be going, and that this time it was going to be a forever home.

To everyone's delight, Boogie slipped into the home as if it was all meant to be. He adored the female dog and the couple. There was no more unpredictable behaviour because he could be himself. He fitted the family and the family fitted him. In the case of Boogie, it really was about looking at the true personality and finding a family to match.

Depression This is one of those areas of communication that breaks my heart. Depression in dogs can be awful, sometimes to the extent that they won't eat, go out, interact with humans or have any real life worth living. It is so sad to see. Depression may be the result of the human owner dying or going into a residential home, the loss of another dog, or a change of family. The number of possible reasons is huge, but in my experience as a communicator it is normally caused by the loss of something or someone.

Seek veterinary help initially to make sure there are no underlying health issues and that the dog really is suffering from depression. I have had numerous call-outs to dogs who were supposedly depressed but were in fact very ill. Pain does not always make dogs cry. They may show their discomfort through being quiet and losing interest in life. So always have the dog checked by a vet first.

If the vet has cleared the dog of a medical condition, the first thing I do is explain to the dog what has happened, using communication and visualisation. So often the dog has no idea where his friend, be it human or animal, has gone. They are often just taken out of a situation and placed with a new family or carer, which can be so heartbreaking for them. Some even think they are being punished for some reason.

Always tell the dog what has happened and why he finds himself in the position he is in. Ask him to accept his new family and tell him that they are there to take good care of him and love him. Allow the dog to grieve, if need be. And think about introducing a new dog friend for support and comfort.

When a dog can understand why he is in a strange home or why his circumstances have changed, he will begin to accept and move forward. The length of time the depression takes to lift varies for each individual dog, but it's usually pretty quick once the dog knows what is happening.

A good natural remedy such as Bach Flower Remedies, healing such as Rieki and so on can also help to heal the emotional trauma dogs can experience. Speak to your vet about finding a good qualified therapist.

Sugar was a classic example of a depressed dog. A small white maltipoo (a cross between a Maltese terrier and a toy poodle), she and her sister Tilly had spent just over ten years together. They were inseparable, and spent hours and hours cleaning each other, playing together and sleeping together. They did everything together.

And then Tilly suffered massive heart failure early one morning and sadly passed away. Sugar was left by her side, waiting for her human mum and dad to wake up and notice her sister had died.

The shock to everyone was devastating but it was worst of all for Sugar. Over the coming days she didn't eat and would barely drink. She stayed in her bed, not moving, and wouldn't even lift up her head. Nothing the family could do would bring her round. She was slipping deeper and deeper into a depressive state.

This is something I deal with a lot in my work. I was called in after she had seen a vet and I explained to the owners that, just like humans, dogs need time for grieving. This is most important.

I sent Sugar lovely images through visualisation of the two of them playing together, and then of Sugar bright and happy on her own, enjoying life as she had done before, when Tilly was with her. I did this every day over the course of a week, and combined the visualisation with spoken words explaining what had happened to Tilly and that it wasn't her fault. I told her that, whilst it was very sad, everything would be fine and she would have the courage to go on happily in life without Tilly's company.

Sure enough, by the end of the week's sessions, Sugar had regained her health and vitality. To everyone's joy, she became a normal dog again.

Sometimes you just need to allow dogs to grieve, as you would allow a human to do, whilst always reassuring them that everything will be OK. In Sugar's case she was able to be happy without her best friend, Tilly.

Rehoming your dog Even from a very early age, I heard people say, 'Oh, that person rehomed their dog! Can you believe it?' Well, at first you would probably agree and say that it just isn't the right thing to do, but I have to disagree with this. Over the years as a professional Animal Communicator I have come across animals that just do not fit the family that they are in and develop all sorts of issues. Once the home has changed, they become a new, happy dog!

Some people feel that, no matter how unhappy they are with each other, it just isn't right to give up. I say we need to be honest with ourselves. Look at the situation from the dog's point of view and ask yourself, Could he or she be happier somewhere else? If the answer is yes, then you really need to think about making that move. If you love your dog, you should be willing to make him happy in whatever way it takes.

I would have loved to keep the lurchers that I rescued, but I knew, realistically, I could not give them the attention, the time and the TLC that each dog needed to help it get over its trauma. I asked myself the question, What would be the best for them? and the answer wasn't what I wanted to hear, but it was the truth. Living with me was not the best option. And so, even though I was heartbroken, I did what was right and found them each the perfect home. I did it for them. It was a selfless act of love but, in the end, I have felt more satisfaction in knowing they are happy than worrying about my own feelings. (I also offered to take the lurchers back at any time, if needed. So I know they will always have me if any unexpected changes happen.)

So you really do need to decide for yourself. You can ask your dog, 'Do you want to stay here?' but be prepared for whatever he tells you. It may not be the answer you wanted to hear, but I would say you already knew that anyway.

There is nothing wrong with rehoming any dog so long as you do it with love, kindness and the dog's interests at heart. If done correctly, rehoming your dog can be a positive step. Go with your gut instincts about the new family, but do your homework first. Do house checks and make sure your dog totally matches the family. Watch how your dog reacts with them, and maybe do a trial run so he gets used to being away from you for a few weeks. See how quickly he settles.

Once you have made the decision and he moves for good, do not keep returning to visit. This can be really upsetting for the dog involved, often creating a feeling of anxiety. You can keep in contact on the phone or by email or letter, but do not visit. Allow him to settle into the family's own routine.

Purdy was a very large, beautiful, orange and black stripy dog, with a huge black nose and amazing amber-coloured eyes. This dog was his owners' pride and joy. There was no doubt that his human mum and dad both adored him. However, after fourteen good years together, the couple had decided it was time to end their relationship as they had grown apart. The man was going to work abroad and couldn't take Purdy where he was going and the woman was moving into a one-bedroom apartment that didn't allow dogs. It was devastating for both of them, but neither were in a position to keep a dog. So the heartbreaking decision was made that Purdy was to be rehomed.

The new home would have to be a lively, energetic, fun-filled place that was ready for a crazy dog! Purdy was not an average dog. He was an unusually bouncy, energetic dog who never stopped playing, and he certainly wasn't for the faint-hearted. Purdy's human mum and dad both worked hard to make sure that the correct home was found, and I was asked to let Purdy know exactly what was happening. So I sent a number of detailed images to him, through visualisation, explaining the rehoming process.

After many enquiries from homes that were not suitable, a lady and her husband who were looking for exactly Purdy's type of large, lively dog popped up. They already had a huge young dog who was very active, and wished to find him a companion he could play with. Their email stood out instantly from the rest of the applications to be Purdy's new owners. Call it gut feeling or intuition, this family seemed right. The owners knew it instantly, and so did I.

It was arranged that Purdy would meet the family at their place the following morning. The visit lasted for a few hours, giving him time to be in the house and play with the other dog. My job was to tell Purdy what was happening and to ask him to be a good boy. Purdy's owners both agreed that if he didn't like the new home they would carry on looking for somewhere else.

They arrived at the house and it was as if Purdy already knew the family. He bounded in and licked the other dog right on the nose. The two of them galloped out through the open patio doors and into the garden, playing tug of war with an old coloured rag bone. Purdy certainly felt at home. The communication I gave him had let him know what was happening, which made him more accepting. And he adored the other dog. When he finally came back into the house, he dived on the new family, landing wet kisses all over them.

That first visit was a great success, and after a few more visits and a weekend stay, Purdy moved in with the new family full-time. He settled happily, as if he had never been anywhere else. This wasn't because he didn't love his old owners. It was because the rehoming had been done correctly. Purdy understood why he was moving to a new home, and the correct personality match was found. He was a very happy dog indeed, and so too were his old owners, who were able to move forward with their new lives, knowing they had done what was best for Purdy.

With all of the above problems, alternative therapies such as Bach Flower Remedies, hands-on healing, Reiki healing and other holistic alternatives can enhance what you are already doing. Ask your vet to recommend some local practitioners.

Chapter Eight

There are so many ways in which I am lucky, and teaching others how to communicate with their pets is one of the most enjoyable things I do. Today, I am probably one of the leading teachers in this field, having been at the forefront of Animal Communication for many years. And I have taught many of the professional communicators now working here in the UK and overseas.

Animal Communication is one of the most natural abilities that we possess. We all have this amazing built-in skill which allows us to achieve interspecies communication, and that includes you! Having taught thousands of people, I am in no doubt that everyone can learn. You, too, can find out what your dog is feeling, thinking and needing by this simple, easy-to-follow process. In this last chapter, I would like to help you develop your own intuitive skills, using some of my Home Study exercises and other knowledge I teach in my workshops. Trust me, it's easy. Let me show you how it's done.

In my experience, we are able to communicate with animals quite freely in childhood, but this ability slowly diminishes as we approach adulthood, when our elders and society tell us it's simply not possible. How many times have you seen children chatting away with an animal, totally enveloped in that moment of connection, when their mother or father tells them, 'Don't be silly, it's just a dog! He can't understand what you are saying.'

Wrong! It is not just a dog (or a cat or any animal, for that matter). He or she is a living, breathing, sentient being that is more than capable of feeling, hurting, mourning, laughing, loving and having all the other emotions, just as we do. Yes, it is an animal, but animals can still communicate. They are not stupid or dumb. They do know what we say, and they try to communicate with us all the time.

Thankfully, though, we are beginning to understand that we have not lost our sixth sense. Our inner abilities are still with us, and they just need to be reawakened. Once you find that childhood innocence again, you will, slowly but surely, see your natural ability to talk with the dogs and other animals return.

Like a muscle, this ability will become stronger and more efficient the more you work it. You wouldn't run a marathon without training first, so be patient. Take it slowly and enjoy the journey, as I take you through the process of learning how communication works. With practice, you will be able to create the correct frequency with your own dog. Watch your connection grow beyond your belief. It will probably change your life with your dog for ever.

Many of us doubt our own abilities. We find it difficult to believe that we are capable of something so amazing as communicating with animals. We may have been told by others that we are not good enough, or that we have limits and that such a feat is totally impossible. Well, trust me, I have taught so many people who doubted they could do it, and every single one could! Everyone is capable of speaking with animals, and I mean everyone. The truth is, once you know how to do it, it's as simple as making a telephone call to a friend – only it's free!

When I introduce myself and say, 'Hi, my name is Joanne and I am a pet psychic', the most common look on people's faces is probably one of horror! They are initially terrified, scared of their own shadow, scared that I might see ghostly figures standing next to them or that I know what they have been getting up to.

Or, on the other hand, I may get 'that look'. You know, the winced one. The face screw-up and the snigger.

Either way, what these people don't realise is that everyone has a psychic ability. We use it every day. It's not scary, nor is it made up. It's a natural form of communication that we all use.

Being psychic simply means using your inner sense, your intuition or gut feeling, if you like, to connect with another person or animal. Mediumship, on the other hand, is an ability to see spirit. When you connect with an animal that has passed, you are using both your psychic and mediumship abilities. You will not suddenly start seeing dead people if you develop your psychic ability, so fear not.

First, let's try this little exercise. Answer each of the following questions either Yes or No.

Your Psychic Exercise

1. Have you ever sensed your dog was trying to tell you something?
   Yes ☐   No ☐

2. Have you ever dreamed of your dog?
   Yes ☐   No ☐

3. With a close family member or friend, do you ever have telepathic flashes?
   Yes ☐   No ☐

4. Have you ever 'known' something was about to happen, and then it did?
Yes ☐   No ☐

5. As a child, did you feel a greater connection with animals than you do today?
Yes ☐   No ☐

6. Do you think your dog can read your mind sometimes?
Yes ☐   No ☐

7. Do you recall your dreams clearly and in detail?
Yes ☐   No ☐

8. Have you suddenly thought about a long-lost friend, and then they called?
Yes ☐   No ☐

9. Are there a lot of coincidences in your life?
Yes ☐   No ☐

10. Do you feel you have an internal guidance in your life?
Yes ☐   No ☐

11. Do you ever feel an animal's physical pain and symptoms of illness in your own body?
Yes ☐   No ☐

12. Have you ever had a feeling you should do or should have done something, and then found out that your feeling was correct?
Yes ☐   No ☐

13. Have you ever seen a picture that a dog has sent you in your mind's eye?
Yes ☐   No ☐

14. Can you accurately guess your dog's emotion?
Yes ☐   No ☐

15. Are your first impressions usually accurate?
Yes ☐   No ☐

For each Yes answer, score 1; for each No answer, score 0. Then total your points and refer to the psychic assessment below.

If you scored **10–15**, your psychic ability is very high already, and it's likely you could develop to the highest standard. You could progress rapidly in Animal Communication with your dog, if you want to.

If you scored **6–9**, you have above-average psychic abilities and potential, and you could develop your ability with practice and discipline. Remember, it's your choice to open your heart to your own potential. Don't let anyone stop you.

If you scored **3–5**, you have experienced your psychic ability, but you need to learn to relax if you wish to develop further. Your potential is there if you want it.

If you scored **0–2**, maybe you are just being a little bit self-critical. Try some meditation to help calm your active mind. Relax and tune in!

I have written a little about psychic awareness so you will learn not to be scared. The media are sometimes confused about the word 'psychic', mistaking it for something it isn't. As we discover what it actually means, you will feel truly happy to be a naturally gifted psychic.

Let's look at the three types of psychic ability – clairvoyance, clairaudience and clairsentience – so you understand what they mean and are not afraid of them. As we begin to use these ways of connecting with people and animals, we are able to look beyond our physical limitations and recognise that we all have boundless creative potential. We rediscover the power of the divine universe that lives within us all and learn how we can release our untapped skills.

Clairvoyance (French for 'clear seeing' or 'clear vision') is the ability to see images not normally perceived. This may refer to pictures or videos in the mind, or simply to a sense of knowing.

I bet there has been an instance when you knew the phone was about to ring. And not only that, I bet you also knew who was going to be on the other end. Yes? Well, that's clairvoyance.

Or when you knew you shouldn't have taken the car out that night, and of course it broke down on your journey. That's clairvoyance.

You may have been thinking about a long-lost friend and then, 'out of the blue', you bumped into them. Clairvoyance again.

You might have insisted your baby was poorly, the doctor said he wasn't but you persevered, and eventually the doctor realised he had missed something and in fact your baby was ill. *Voilà!* Clairvoyance.

When such instances occur, we feel comfortable saying 'It was a gut feeling' or 'I just knew', and that is perfectly fine, of course. But do we ever think it's psychic?

The connection we have with some people is so strong that we call the feeling of knowing telepathy. I often experience it with my sister. For instance, I could be thinking about a dress I have seen and have the image in my mind – the shape, style, colour and detail – and my sister will already have the clear image in her mind too. This is pure telepathy, but we all have this ability. Perhaps we notice it more with those who are closest to us.

The best news is that this is not just something that

connects human to human. No, telepathy can happen between all animal species, which means that we can have telepathic communication with dogs and other animals too. And not only that, but they can do it back!

Clairaudience ('clear hearing') is an inner hearing that can include sounds as well as words.

This happens to most people, but it is often lost in our internal chatter. When you learn to turn down your chatter, the words will stay. It's like tuning in to a particular frequency on the radio.

One of the ways of hearing what you normally miss is to be quiet and listen. Turn your TV off. (OK, I realise that some of you love your favourite soaps and films, but compromise. Maybe choose a time every day when you have a TV- or radio-free hour.) Give yourself a quiet time, just for you and your inner self.

Many people who study different forms of meditation adore this time, the time for inner peace. When I choose to quieten my life down, my clairaudience kicks in big time. Sometimes even I am surprised at how amazing it can be.

In the first few days of quietness, your thoughts and inner voice will open up like a butterfly spreading its wings for the first time. You will soon be able to observe what you are thinking, as if you are standing to one side, detached and able to take stock of your thoughts from a different perspective. Enjoy finding yourself, your true inner self.

Clairsentience ('clear feeling') is the realm of kinesthetic feeling. This can include extreme emotional feelings, as well as taste, smell and other physical sensations.

This is the most common form of psychic connection. At some point everyone will pick up on feelings, emotions or energy.

How many times have you walked into a crowded room and instantly been drawn to people whom you know you will like? Maybe you feel they look familiar, even though you have never met them. On the other hand, what about those with whom you immediately feel uneasy? We are all capable of picking up on the energy or frequency levels of other people.

And it is no different when working with your dog. You will instantly pick up and feel its emotion. For instance, your dog may be looking perfectly well in the physical sense, but the feelings you are picking up might tell a different story. You may feel unhappy, even emotional to the point of tears. Then you can find out what the problem is by asking the dog questions.

And you can gain more awareness about your own

feelings by asking yourself, How do I feel? Why am I upset? What makes me unhappy? You will end up with the answers you need instantly.

When I teach my workshops, more than half my students 'feel' the animal's energy. Most end up crying, and have absolutely no idea why. It's because they are using their energy in a clairsentient way. It's a new way of feeling.

Guess what? You are psychic!!! Still scared? No, of course you're not, because it all makes sense.

So now let me teach you how to communicate with your dog using my methods. Let's start at the beginning.

In order to hear what our dogs are trying to say, we first need to relax. Day-to-day jibber-jabber will affect our ability to hear them. Our dogs and all other animals have a frequency, almost like an internal radio. In order to tune into that frequency, we must first quiet our own internal radio.

Imagine two wavy frequency lines, the top one being ours and the bottom one being the animal's. We can communicate with the animal when our frequency top line relaxes and merges down with the dog's bottom one. This is when we get what I call the love link, a simple connection of two frequencies. (Animals naturally have a higher frequency than humans, but for the learning process I like to switch it round so that it is easier to understand.)

Most people find communication easy if they are relaxed and in a quiet state of mind when they are connecting with an animal. I suppose the big question is, How do I relax enough to hear my dog? With all our daily activities, worries and jobs that need doing, we must take time out in order to relax and quiet the mind. Here is a simple exercise to try:

Find yourself a quiet time. Turn off the TV and any other noise, if you can.

Take a moment and just breathe. Relax your whole body.

Now visualise the first dog that stole your heart. Just keep the image in your mind for a moment or two.

Think about the dog's coat – what colour is it?

Now see the dog's paws, visualise them – what do they look like?

Move to his/her face – notice his/her nose.

Now look into the eyes – how do they make you feel? Do you feel the love?

Breathe in the dog. Allow yourself to just be with him/her. Notice how he/she makes you feel.

Take a deep breath and bring your focus back to reality.

Isn't it strange that, when you focus on your love of the dog, you completely forget about all the other issues in your life? It's as if your heart truly opens up to another place.

If you have a little time, you might like to have a go at this short meditation. Although meditation isn't completely necessary for communication, it is a great starting point when learning the process. You will find that it becomes easier to relax and find yourself in a place of calm.

Whilst doing the meditation exercise, why not keep your notepad and pen next to you, and make a note of any words, feelings, pictures or even messages that may come to you from your dog before you start asking your questions?

You may wish to read this through first or, as some people do, record yourself reading it through and then play it back to yourself.

Here I have added another exercise that you could do. As everyone is individual, I suggest you have a go at both exercises, then choose the one that you feel most comfortable with for future use. Both of these are designed for relaxation.

Lie or sit in a comfortable position, with your dog close by you or in the same room.

Close your eyes and just breathe. Notice each breath, and the rise and fall of your chest. Spend a couple of minutes focusing on your breathing.

Start at the top of your head and breathe in. As you exhale, blow away any tension and breathe out any aches and pains.

Now work your way down to your throat area, then your chest area, your tummy, hips, legs, knees and feet. You now feel completely relaxed. Just breathe.

Imagine you are walking through a beautiful field. You are barefoot and can feel the dewy grass under your feet. Notice how this feels. Can you see what you are wearing? Is it all in colour?

The sun is shining. You feel radiant, happy and relaxed, but most of all you feel free. No stress, no worries. Just free.

You begin to smell the sweet scent of the flowers that surround you. You hear the birds in the trees. You are now back with nature. This is where you feel safe. You feel secure and at peace.

You look ahead and notice a figure in the distance. It is not human but animal. Although it's quite far away, you can still see what the animal looks like.

You are overwhelmed with love, and fear nothing.

As the animal comes closer you feel such warmth of unconditional love that you feel totally relaxed and at peace.

As he approaches you he offers you something. It's a small heart-shaped pendant. Notice what colour it is, what it looks like and how it feels in your hand.

Thank the animal guide who gave you the pendant. He nods his head at you in respect and his image slowly disappears in front of you.

Feeling wonderfully relaxed and at peace, begin walking back through the field. Bring your focus back to your breathing. Notice how your body rises and falls with each breath.

Bring yourself back by working your breathing from your feet up to your knees, legs, hips, tummy, chest, then neck and finally head.

Open your eyes . . . You are wide awake and feeling relaxed and refreshed. You are full of happiness and love.

Feel good? I bet you do.

Use this exercise whenever you feel a bit stressed or before you do a reading with your dog, if you need to calm down a little.

The pendant is the gift of communication. Whenever you feel doubt about your ability, you just need to think about the pendant and how it looks and this will trigger your new communication skills with your dog. You will find it easy to receive information and be able to hear the dog's thoughts clearly.

You may want to write down what the animal guide looked like in the back of your notepad. Was he what you thought he would be? And after you have done this exercise a few more times, did he change? Or say anything to you? Write it all down. It can be an incredible experience in itself.

When you first start to learn communication with your dog, it is inevitable that you will doubt your ability. In the beginning you may feel as if you are making up the information you receive. It can be difficult to distinguish between what is real and what is made up. The logical side of your brain will convince you that the information is a hoax and your mind is playing tricks on you.

There are two reasons for this. Firstly, you are talking with your own dog, and you already have a lot of information about him or her, including their likes, dislikes and habits.

And secondly, the voice you hear may well be your own, because the animal will send its thoughts to you and your own voice will deliver them. This is why you may feel you have made the information up. Overcoming these doubts can be hard but, with practice, you will be able to tell the difference between what's real and what's not. Trust in your dog and listen carefully to what you get.

You may hear your dog in voice, your own voice translating their words. You may hear them in emotion, in picture form or even as a video playback in your mind. You may experience one of the above or all of them. Everyone is different. There are no rules. What happens is individual to you.

I like to say to my students, 'Please don't grow arms and legs on your torso of information!' When you receive some information from your dog your brain will often want to put in a background picture. Say your dog sends you a mind picture of a bucket and spade, your brain will immediately add a beach with the sea, and maybe some seagulls and sandcastles. But actually, you only saw a bucket and spade! Learning to use the information that your dog sends you, without turning it into something it isn't, is key to getting answers from your dog.

The way to do this is easy. When you do a reading with your pet, you should always have a pen and paper with you. I encourage you to decorate your notepad with personal things you like. (For instance, I have covered mine with photographs of my late poodle Mr Klein. Just seeing his little face on my notepad makes me smile and encourages me to trust what I receive from the animal I am working with.) Always write your answers down as soon as the information pops into your mind. That way the information will be on paper and cannot be changed.

When you begin to communicate with your dog, the information often comes into your heart and mind very fast, almost at the speed of lightning! Sometimes you get answers before you have actually finished asking your question. This is perfectly normal. Just write the information down and accept it graciously.

Please remember always to be totally honest with yourself. Follow your heart, intuition, gut feeling and emotions. The more you trust what you get, the easier it will be for the information to find you.

Don't be tempted to guess. Your psychic ability will get better the more you practise. If you start cheating, the only person you are defrauding is yourself.

Thinking of questions to ask your dog is one of the hardest things to do when you start, so let me help you a little.

Whilst you may think you already know the answers, you might just be surprised at what your dog actually thinks. Most are worth asking anyway, and you can tailor your questions for your own dog. Be creative. The more questions you ask, the more information you will get. Here are some suggestions:

- Who's your best friend? (Don't be upset if it's not you)
- Do you have a favourite place to sleep?
- Do you like your name?
- What are your favourite activities?
- Do you like children?
- Describe your personality to me.
- What do you like?
- What do you dislike?
- Do you like other animals of different species?
- Is there anything you need or want in life?
- Which people do you especially like?
- Is there anything you wish to tell me or that I need to know?
- Where do you like to go for a walk best?
- Do you like going to your obedience class?
- Do you like cats?
- Are you happy to be in the company of other dogs?

- Do you like to ride in the car?
- Do you like it when you go on holiday?
- Did you enjoy going to the seaside?
- Have you ever had puppies? (This question is for females, perhaps if your dog is a rescue)
- Do you like water?
- Do you enjoy playing with a ball or toy?

Also think of some questions that will give you validation. Perhaps ask the dog to tell you a secret or something that he has recently overheard one of the other family members saying. It needs to be something you will be able to validate, to prove you are actually speaking with him and not making it all up. This is when you can be creative with your questioning. (You may very well be totally shocked at the information your dog gives you and that the information is correct!)

Now you have an idea of the questions you'd like to ask, you can start the communication exercise. It is best to do this when no one else is around, so that you will not have any interruptions.

Sit quietly on a chair or sofa and relax, with your dog sitting beside you or near to you, also relaxed. If you can relax, you are halfway there. Use the relaxation or meditation exercises given above if you are finding this difficult.

Close your eyes, breathe slowly and steadily, blow all your cares and worries out into the atmosphere to clear your body of all negativity. You can do this breathing exercise for however long feels right for you. Relax totally and surround your body and your dog in a pink light of love and protection.

Now look at your gorgeous dog. Notice the coat texture and colour, his body, eyes, nose and the shape of his ears, perhaps his tail. In other words, fall in love all over again. Spend a minute or so just soaking up the love and beauty of him.

In your first few conversations with your dog, you might wish to try and visualise your two auras merging. By 'aura', I mean the energy surrounding you both. Auras surround all living things, appearing a few feet from the body. They are pure energy and can change colour at different times, reflecting your emotional, physical and mental disposition. Imagine the two interlinking, as the diagram opposite shows. (There are many books available on the subject of auras, which are worth exploring and understanding.)

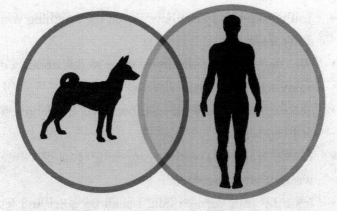

Once you visualise these auras merging, take three deep breaths and simply ask your dog, 'Will you communicate with me?'

You will hear the word 'yes' or 'perhaps' or 'maybe' or even something else, or you might see the words in your mind's eye. You may even become emotional and filled with love. If any of the above happens, you have your answer. (Remember, it may come through as if you have just spoken to yourself. It's your own voice translating, so this is normal. Trust and go with it.)

Send your animal love, and tell him or her that you are willing to see, hear and feel absolutely anything, using one or two of the following sentences:

- You can share with me as little or as much as you like. It's up to you.

- You absolutely do not have to tell me anything you don't want to.

- We can talk about what you want to talk about. I'd enjoy that very much.

- Tell me what you wish to know. I will be as honest as I can for you.

- I will graciously receive anything you give me without any judgement.

- It's now your turn to talk. I shall be quiet and let you tell me what I need to know. I love you.

By doing this, you are showing you can be trusted. To keep the connection open, always respect the animal and have gratitude for their co-operation. They are putting their trust in you.

Now ask your questions, and listen out for the answers. Look at your dog, but do not stare. Just relax your thoughts onto the dog. This will allow your heart to make the love link, when you and your dog connect through love, making communication possible.

When you have finished asking all your questions and writing down your answers, thank your dog for his or her communication.

Focus on bringing your body back to itself. Hear your own breathing, place your hand on your heart and visualise it beating. Bring your attention back to yourself.

Become aware of the feelings, emotions and sensations in your own body. Although you and your dog sometimes share experiences, you are both separate and unique energy-filled sentient beings.

Visualise a beautiful pink shimmering light surrounding your dog. It is full of love and protection.

Now visualise the same beautiful light surrounding your own body too, from head to toe. Enjoy this for a moment or two.

Wow! You have done it.

Now have a look at what you received. Was it what you expected? Is there anything your dog wanted you to know? Can you do something to make his life better?

When your dog begins to trust your communication, he or she will put you to the test. They will see what you do with the information they send you. You may have proved that you hear them and love them unconditionally, but they will watch to see that you further prove this through your actions.

For instance, if your dog tells you that he would really like you to stop putting the sprinkles of vegetables on top of his dinner in the evening, you must do so. Or perhaps he asks you to move his bed away from the window area so he's not in a cold draught. You may prefer it placed there, as it is out of your way, but you must listen and do as he asks. To gain your dog's trust, you must (within reason) follow through with action.

Remember, you can talk with your dog at any time. In fact, the more you communicate with him, the easier it will become and the happier and more content your dog will be.

Tracking uses communication to find missing animals. You can use your communication love link to connect with the animal via a photograph, just as you would if you were tuning in to a pet who has passed over.

This is one of the best ways to find out information on the health and whereabouts of a dog. If the dog is quite intelligent, he could describe road signs and buildings, or tell you whether or not he is hungry or has already eaten. If he's not so intelligent (because, just like humans, some dogs are intelligent and some are not), you could at least find out in which direction he went.

It's not always easy to connect with a missing dog, but it can be a valuable tool when it goes right. Use it alongside the traditional methods of looking for pets who have gone missing.

Time is of the essence, so the earlier you get on to finding your dog the better. Here's what to do if your dog goes missing:

- Try not to panic. This is easier said than done, but you really need to try and stay focused so that you work like a military expert, covering as many options as possible.
- Contact police stations within a five-mile radius of the place where your dog went missing.
- Ask all your immediate neighbours if they have seen your dog.
- Post flyers in the neighbourhood and within a five-mile radius of where your dog went missing.
- Contact all the animal homes, humane societies and veterinary clinics within a five-mile radius of where the animal went missing. If possible, give them a flyer with a photo of your dog, so he will be easy to recognise.
- Ask friends and people you know who work with healing to pray for the safe return of the animal.
- Post posters and updates on a social network site such as Facebook.
- And please, ASAP, contact www.dogslost.co.uk, which operates here in the UK.

When your dog goes missing, it's natural to think of the worst situations that he or she must be in. Try hard not to do this. I recommend my clients to visualise their dog being reunited with them. Instead of focusing on him being gone, imagine the meeting when you find him. See yourself greeting your loved dog with a huge smile, your heart filled with love and thanks for his safe return.

And please, if he isn't already, get him microchipped! Ask your vet for details.

If your dog isn't found quickly, try using communication to help or enhance your search. The sooner communication is used the better. Have a photo of your dog to hand and tune in to your love link just as you would if you were doing a normal communication with him. Here are some questions to ask a missing dog:

- Are you injured?
- What can you see? (Landmarks, house numbers, schools, bridges, street signs, shop signs, drains, water, ditches, and so on)
- What can you smell?
- When you left your home, what was the last thing you saw?
- Which door did you go out of?
- Did you turn left or right?

- Show me your journey.
- What did you see?
- What did you feel?
- What is under your paws? Can you show me?
- Have you seen other animals?
- Can you please stay safe, keep away from traffic.
- How many dark nights have passed since you left home?
- Are you thirsty?
- Are you hungry?
- What have you eaten?
- Have you found any food?
- What was it?
- Are you alone?
- Can you see any humans?
- Are you sheltered at night?
- Are you hiding under something?
- Are you trapped in someone else's territory?
- Do you know how to get home?
- Do you want to go home?
- Why haven't you returned home?
- Why did you leave?

It's so important you listen careful to everything your dog tells you at this time, and if you don't get anything straightaway, don't panic. Just try again later. You can never guarantee tracking will work, but it's certainly worth a go.

When you have all the information that your dog has given you via your communication, hand it over to friends and family or those who are helping you find your dog. You may be surprised at how often people recognise landmarks or road names that your dog was able to give you. This is when you know without a shadow of a doubt that you are tuned in with the dog and that your connection and love link is working.

Remote viewing simply means tuning into your dog whilst you are away from home. This is a great thing to do and something I use an awful lot, as my work schedule takes me away from home so often.

You can use remote viewing to see if your dog is OK and to check that everything you have requested is being done by the carer or your family, or you can just say hello, I love you. For me, the latter is most common, although I sometimes find out if my dogs have been fed on time.

The way to do this is simple. Have a picture of your dog in your mind, create a love link by thinking about them and

then just ask a question, as you would in a normal reading.
I like to ask things such as:

- Are you OK?
- Do you need anything?
- Have you been fed?
- What have you been doing today?

Some questions are really fun, because you can then phone
the person who is looking after your dog and tell them
what you have been told. It often provokes a strange kind
of shock and paranoia because of the accuracy of the
information!

Mirroring is an interesting phenomenon that I and many
other communicators have all witnessed at some stage.
I have often noticed that a high number of dogs have
injuries and illnesses identical to those of the people with
whom they live. I suppose vets and those who work in the
industry have seen it too. Some like to call it 'resonance'.

I can only assume this occurs because the dogs have
heightened empathic feelings for their owners. Because our
lovable, loyal dogs have no barriers with us people, some

may take this too far. Absorbing our emotions can make them emotionally unbalanced themselves, which, for some, can develop into illness. It is as if they are holding up a mirror to show their owner the disharmony, emotional imbalance or disease that is present in their owner's body, giving them a picture of their medical problems and offering the owners a chance to see what is wrong with them. Dogs can even take on negative behaviour. For example, they will often show the same intolerance as their owners towards some people.

One dog I spoke with recently was a little French bulldog called Boogie. His owner had noticed that whenever she had an accident, within days Boogie had one too. He had suffered everything from a broken front leg and a damaged ear to a swollen toe. It was becoming more and more evident that Boogie was mirroring his person.

I spoke with him through communication and explained that it wasn't his job to take on his owner's pain. Instead he must try and stay healthy for his mum to mirror. By switching the role, Boogie was able to become healthy, and his owner got better, too.

If your dog is very close to you emotionally, you may sometimes feel he is mirroring you. It is important to release your dog from this mirroring state. Suggest he let go of your emotions and explain clearly that your feelings are not his to hang on to. Tell your dog that you appreciate what he is doing to help you, but that you need him to be a picture of health, with no illness or disease.

In most cases of mirroring, the animal becomes healed when the owner sorts him or herself out in life.

Troubleshooting
Should I ask my questions out loud?
Well, that is totally up to you. I ask all my questions in my mind and send them as thoughts. Do what feels right for you.

What if my dog won't speak to me?
Highly unlikely, but if this does happen just leave it for that day and try again another time.

What if I get disturbed halfway through?
No problem. Just thank your dog and tell him or her you will carry on another time.

What if I can't relax?
Don't worry. Try the meditation exercise again or listen to some soft music. The worst thing you can do is put yourself under pressure.

I can't hear my dog.
You will. Just make sure you relax. Stop focusing on

hearing and notice how you feel after each question instead.

My dog has asked me for something I cannot give.

In cases such as this, you have to explain to your dog why the request is not possible. Try and find a compromise or alternative option, but always tell your dog why you cannot fulfil his request.

People think I'm mad talking to my dog!

It really does not matter. So long as you stay truthful with the information you receive from your dog, you can develop a unique bond that others may not understand. What you need to remember is that you are doing the best for your dog, and that is all that matters. Don't get into arguments with people who do not understand. Just walk your own path. When they are ready, they will come to you to find out more.

Can I talk with other people's animals?

The answer is yes, of course. But I would strongly advise that you do further training, as working with other people's animals can be tricky. You really do need to understand the various sections of communication. Why not take a look at my website for training opportunities? Details are at the end of this book.

My dog has passed to spirit. Should I still try and communicate?

This is your choice, but dogs that have passed are just as capable of communicating as live animals, and the process is exactly the same. Use a photograph of your dog and adjust the questions as necessary.

I hope that I have given you enough information to help you try communication for yourself. Enjoy every moment and celebrate the fact that you can indeed talk to the animals!

Acknowledgements

I feel so utterly grateful for the precious gift of Animal Communication, and the best bit is being able to share my experiences with all of you. I hope I have inspired you to take time to listen to your animals. They are so keen for you to hear them.

So many animals have guided, taught and encouraged, loved and inspired me throughout the years and I obviously still have a long way to go, as I seem to be learning something new each day. Without a doubt, the animals in my life have helped me become the person I am today. And with my whole-hearted trust, they will take my future work in the direction it needs to go. One thing is for sure, the animals are guiding me into teaching others how to communicate.

I would like to thank you all for your belief in the work I do. None of this would have been possible without the endless encouragement of my agent, Luigi Bonomi, and I am eternally grateful.

This book couldn't have been written without my publishers, Headline, and especially my editor, Carly Cook, who expertly guides me through the twists and turns of the publishing journey, and her team of so many special people behind the scenes. A big thank you from the bottom of my heart.

A very special thank you to all the lovely staff at the beautiful Dakota Hotel in Scotland, where I spent hour upon hour in the lounge on the huge comfy sofa, typing away on my laptop putting this book together, with the unbeatable constant coffee service. I really can't say thank you enough. My sanity, concentration and creative brain were kept intact by the support of you all and the relaxing surroundings of the hotel.

And finally, thank you to all the precious dogs and puppies that my family and I have known, and who have given me, unconditionally, protection in times of fear, comfort in times of need and, above all, love in times of heartache. You have walked with me, shared my tears, sadness and happiness, and touched my heart so deeply. I will always be truly grateful.

To Blackie, Regal, Soba, Lady, Metro, Toona, Pernod, Paris, Paddy, Sally, Mozart, Mosko, Minti, Cassie, Ruben, Rosie and those that crossed our paths just briefly. Last but not least, to my wonderful little poodle Mr Klein. This book is a tribute to you all. Through it, your memory will live on in the hearts of many.

Joanne x

Details of all my workshops and learning opportunities, including a Home Study course, are available through my website, www.joannehull.com

THE PET PSYCHIC

JOANNE HULL

They speak, she listens
Amazing tales from the world of animal communication

Joanne Hull always knew there was something that
made her different from other children.

While other girls her age were playing with dolls,
Joanne was busy collecting any stray animal that came
her way, until her parents' backyard resembled a zoo.
As she grew older she realised that she was developing
incredible powers that allowed her to psychically
connect with, and talk to, animals.

For the last ten years Joanne has used the animal spirit
world to help owners across the country understand
troubled pets, find missing ones and, most amazingly,
contact those we've lost to the other side. Joanne has
given hundreds of spine-chillingly accurate readings –
and for the first time she shares the sometimes
heart-warming, sometimes heart-breaking, but
always extraordinary stories that have formed
her life as The Pet Psychic.

UNTIL TUESDAY

LUIS CARLOS MONTALVÁN
with BRET WITTER

Until Tuesday, Luis Carlos Montalván could barely walk half a mile. Until Tuesday, simply riding the subway was a terrifying ordeal. Luis sometimes struggled just to get out of bed. Because Tuesday isn't just any dog; he's a service dog, specially trained to care for his owner. And with his golden coat and sensitive eyes he's also the kind of dog that you can't help but love.

When Captain Luis Carlos Montalván retired from seventeen years of service in the US army, suffering from physical disabilities, agoraphobia and Post Traumatic Stress, it was Tuesday – a big dog with a beguiling smile – who brought him back from the brink.

This is the moving and inspirational story of how a soldier fought back from the devastation of being injured in action, and how an incredible dog became his protector, his companion and, ultimately, his saviour.

NON-FICTION / MEMOIR 978 0 7553 6188 5

MAKING THE ROUNDS WITH OSCAR

DAVID DOSA

This is the incredible story of Oscar, an otherwise ordinary cat with an almost psychic sensitivity to human beings. As the resident cat of Steere House, an old people's nursing home, he knows before anyone else when people are at the end of their lives. His presence at a patient's bedside is an almost absolute indicator of their impending death, and allows staff members to notify families that the end is near. Oscar is a wonder to the doctors and nurses; he provides companionship to those who would otherwise die alone, and he gives comfort where others have failed.

Dr David Dosa's account of Oscar and his patients is heartfelt, moving, sometimes even funny. *Making the Rounds with Oscar* allows readers into a world rarely seen from the outside.